Top
Dubai
10

explorer

there's more to life...
ask**explorer**.com

C000193504

Dubai Top Ten 2012/1st Edition
ISBN 978-9948-16-825-6

Copyright © Explorer Group Ltd, 2012.
All rights reserved.

Front Cover Photograph – Burj Khalifa – Pete Maloney

Printed and bound by Emirates Printing Press, Dubai, United Arab Emirates.

Explorer Publishing & Distribution
PO Box 34275, Dubai , United Arab Emirates
Phone   +971 (0)4 340 8805
Fax   +971 (0)4 340 8806
Email   info@askexplorer.com
Web   askexplorer.com

Welcome...

...to **Dubai Top 10**, your step-by-step guide to the City of Gold. Dubai is, of course, a city and emirate of superlatives. Whether it's the tallest buildings, biggest malls, most expensive hotels or best views... everything here is bigger, better, faster and more. With so many extremes on offer, it can be hard to know which ones to head for.

So, this book is your handy little guide to which must-sees you absolutely, well, must see during your visit to this fascinating emirate. In total, we've listed 100 of Dubai's very best, divided into 10 categories that range from supreme showstopper restaurants to essential family days out, from cracking cultural attractions to the city's very best bars – and plenty more in-between. From number one to number ten, they're in no particular order, so make sure you try to get around as many as possible.

And, as we always like to give our readers that little bit extra, you'll also find the top 10 places to visit outside of Dubai, as well as lists of the top 10 malls, 10 not-to-miss golf courses and 10 child-friendly restaurants and cafes that the whole family will love.

So, whether you're visiting Dubai for a day, a week, a month, or maybe even longer, there's no excuse for not seeing the very best that the city, and the United Arab Emirates, has to offer.

For even more inspiration, **askexplorer.com** is jam-packed with tips for the latest happenings and openings in the UAE and beyond.

Happy holidaying,

The Explorer Team

there's more to life...
ask**explorer**.com

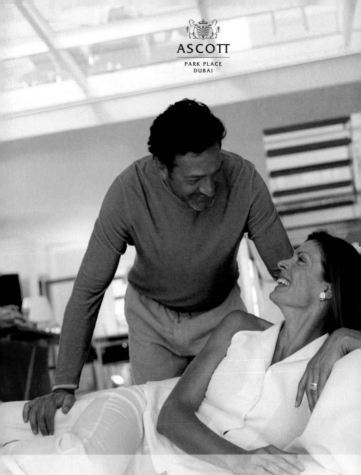

ASCOTT
PARK PLACE
DUBAI

Experience Exclusive Global Living

Stay along the exclusive Sheikh Zayed Road. Ascott Park Place Dubai provides luxury residences overlooking magnificent views of the city, with comprehensive services and modern facilities in the iconic Park Place Tower. Indulge in our 40-metre temperature controlled swimming pool, work out in our state-of-the-art gymnasium or unwind in our steam & sauna rooms. Relax, recharge and stay at your peak with us. **Because life is about living.**

Managed by

THE
ASCOTT
LIMITED

A Member of CapitaLa

For further information and global reservations, please visit www.the-ascott.co **call (971) 4310 8555 or email enquiry.dubai@the-ascott.com**

Ascott Park Place Dubai is managed by The Ascott Limited, a member of CapitaLand. It is the largest global serviced residence owner-operator in Asia Pacific, Europe and the Gulf region, managing the *Ascott*, *Citadines* and *Somerset* brands in over 70 cities across more than 20 countries.

SHAKESPEARE AND CO.

Café Restaurant - Pâtisserie - Chocolates - Catering - Flowers

Drink Coca-Cola

DUBAI

The Village
04 344 6228

Al Attar Business Tower
04 331 1757

Souk Al Bahar
04 425 7971

Dubai Marina Mall
04 457 4199

Al Manzil Flowers
04 422 4562

Safa Center
04 394 1121

Arabian Ranches
04 447 0444

Dubai Mall
04 434 0195

Emirates Hills
04 360 8886

Etihad Mall
04 284 3749

ABU DHABI

Guardian Towers,
Al Rehham Area
02 491 7673

Central Market Mall
02 639 9626

AL AIN

Al Ain Mall
03 764 83 16

RAS AL KHAIMAH

Al Hamra Mall
07 243 4660

Catering

catering@shakespeareandco.ae
+971 043291040

Flowers

flowershop@shakespeareandco.ae
+971 043291040

Pâtisserie

Available at all locations

Coming Soon
Deerfields. Abu Dhabi
Yas Island. Abu Dhabi
Paragon Bay. Abu Dhabi
Matajer Al Juraina. Sharjah

Contents

ask**explorer**.com

Since 1996, **explorer** has been the UAE's Number 1 source for all the information you need about living life under the Gulf sun to the fullest.

With some 150 much-loved products in our portfolio, we cover every aspect of life in the Middle East: from off-road adventures to career advice, there's a guide to match all interests – get yours today at **askexplorer.com/shop**.

And for even more insider tips and inspiration, including details of the latest happenings in Dubai, Abu Dhabi and beyond, **askexplorer.com** has all the answers.

Welcome To
Dubai

Welcome to a city of stark contrasts; of sand dunes and skyscrapers, camels and fast cars, museums and malls. Welcome to Dubai.

Whatever your reason for touching down in this desert metropolis, it's hard not to be captivated by its growth and unshakeable ambition. The world's tallest building is already here, and a slew of architectural wonderpieces and whole new communities are not far behind.

Yet, underneath the shiny surface, there is more to Dubai than cranes and five-star cliches: you'll find Emiratis, cosmopolitan expats and sunburnt tourists, all enjoying and exploring the many aspects of a surprisingly multilayered city. As you'd expect from a truly international destination, there is a wide scope of activities, cuisines and adventures to be had, many at prices you wouldn't expect from the 'seven-star' headlines.

Culture & Heritage

Development Of Islam
Islam developed in modern-day Saudi Arabia at the beginning of the seventh century AD with the revelations of the Quran being received by the Prophet Muhammad. Military conquests of the Middle East and North Africa enabled the Arab Empire to spread the teachings of Islam to the local Bedouin tribes. Following the Arab Empire, the Turks, the Mongols and the Ottomans all left their marks on local culture.

The Trucial States
After the fall of the Muslim empires, both the British and Portuguese became interested in the area due to its strategic position between India and Europe. A series of maritime

truces took place, and Dubai and the other emirates accepted British protection in 1892. In Europe, the area became known as the Trucial Coast (or Trucial States), a name it retained until the departure of the British in 1971.

Growing Trade
In the late 1800s, Dubai's ruler, Sheikh Maktoum bin Hasher Al Maktoum, granted tax concessions to foreign traders, encouraging many to switch their operations from Iran and Sharjah to Dubai. By 1903, a British shipping line had been persuaded to use Dubai as its main port in the area, giving traders direct links with British India and other key ports. Dubai's importance as a trading hub was further enhanced by Sheikh Rashid bin Saeed Al Maktoum, father of the current ruler, who ordered the creek to be dredged to provide access for larger vessels. The city came to specialise in the import and re-export of goods, mainly gold to India, and trade became the foundation of the emirate's wealthy progression.

Independence
In 1968, Britain announced its withdrawal from the region and oversaw the proposed creation of a single state. The ruling sheikhs, particularly of Abu Dhabi and Dubai, realised that by uniting forces they would have a stronger voice in the wider Middle East region. In 1971, the federation of the United Arab Emirates was born.

Formation Of The UAE
The new state comprised the emirates of Dubai, Abu Dhabi, Ajman, Fujairah,

Sharjah, Umm Al Quwain and, in 1972, Ras Al Khaimah. The individual emirates each retain a degree of autonomy, with Abu Dhabi and Dubai providing the most input into the federation. The leaders of the new federation elected the ruler of Abu Dhabi, HH Sheikh Zayed bin Sultan Al Nahyan, to be their president, a position he held until he passed away on 2 November 2004. His eldest son, HH Sheikh Khalifa bin Zayed Al Nahyan, was then elected president.

The Discovery Of Oil

The UAE's formation came after the discovery of huge oil reserves in Abu Dhabi in 1958. The emirate has an incredible 10% of the world's known oil reserves. In 1966, Dubai, already a relatively wealthy trading centre, also discovered oil. Dubai's ruler at the time, the late Sheikh Rashid bin Saeed Al Maktoum, ensured that oil revenues were used to develop an economic and social infrastructure – the basis of today's society. His work was continued through the reign of his son and successor, Sheikh Maktoum bin Rashid Al Maktoum and the present ruler, Sheikh Mohammed bin Rashid Al Maktoum.

Culture

Despite Dubai being a modern metropolis, the emirate is still rooted in its traditions. Courtesy and hospitality are highly prized virtues and visitors are likely to experience the genuine warmth and friendliness of the local people – although less than 15% of the population is Emirati.

The country's rulers are committed to safeguarding its heritage by promoting cultural and sporting events that represent the UAE's traditions, such as falconry, camel racing and traditional dhow sailing. Arabic culture, as seen through poetry, dancing, songs and traditional art, is also encouraged.

Wooden dhows have been sailing from all over the Gulf into Dubai Creek for centuries and, even today, dhow builders continue to make these beautiful vessels using only teak and traditional hand tools. Head to the dhow yards near Al Jaddaf at the top of the creek to watch the masters at work.

Food & Drink

Most of the Arabic food available is based on Lebanese cuisine. Common dishes are shawarma (lamb or chicken carved from a spit and served in a pita bread with salad and tahina), falafel (mashed chickpeas and sesame seeds, rolled into balls and deep fried), hummus (a creamy dip made from chickpeas and olive oil), and tabbouleh (finely chopped parsley, mint and crushed wheat).

Among the most famed Middle Eastern delicacies are dates and coffee. Dates are one of the few crops that thrive naturally throughout the Arab world and date palms have been cultivated in the area for around 5,000 years. Local coffee is mild with a taste of cardamom and saffron, and it is served black without sugar. Muslims are not allowed to eat pork. In order for a restaurant to have pork on its menu, it should have a separate fridge, preparation equipment and cooking area. Supermarkets are also required to sell pork in a separate area. Alcohol is also considered haram (taboo) in Islam. It is only served in licensed outlets associated with hotels (restaurants and bars), plus a few leisure venues (such as golf clubs) and clubs.

Shisha

Smoking the traditional shisha (water pipe) is a popular and relaxing pastime enjoyed throughout the Middle East. Shisha pipes can be smoked with a variety of aromatic flavours, such as strawberry, grape or apple. Contrary to what many people think, shisha tobacco contains nicotine and can be addictive.

Religion

Islam is the official religion of the UAE and is widely practised; however, there are people of various nationalities and religions working and living in the region side by side.

Muslims are required to pray (facing Mecca) five times a day. Most people pray at a mosque, although it's not unusual to see people kneeling by the side of the road if they are not near a place of worship. The call to prayer, transmitted through loudspeakers on the minarets of each mosque, ensures that everyone knows it's time to pray. Friday is the Islamic holy day, and the first day of the weekend in Dubai, when most businesses close to allow people to go to the mosque to pray, and to spend time with their families. Many shops and tourist attractions have different hours of operation, opening around 14:00 after Friday prayers.

During the holy month of Ramadan, Muslims abstain from all food, drinks, cigarettes and inappropriate thoughts (or activities) between dawn and dusk for 30 days. In the evening, the fast is broken with the iftar feast. All over the city, festive Ramadan tents are filled to the brim with people of all nationalities and religions enjoying shisha, traditional Arabic mezze and sweets. The timing of Ramadan is not fixed in terms of the Gregorian calendar, but depends on the lunar Islamic calendar.

National Dress

In general, the local population wears traditional dress in public. For men this is the dishdash(a) or khandura: a white full length shirt dress, which is worn with a white or red checked headdress, known as a gutra. This is secured with a black cord (agal). In public, women wear the black abaya – a long, loose robe that covers their normal clothes – plus a headscarf called a sheyla. The abaya is often of sheer, flowing fabric and may be open at the front. Some women also wear a thin black veil hiding their face and/or gloves, and some older women wear a leather mask, known as a burkha, which covers the nose, brow and cheekbones.

Modern Dubai

People & Economy

There are an estimated 150 nationalities living in Dubai. The population in 1968 was 58,971. By 2010, it had grown to 1.9 million, according to Dubai Statistics Center. However, the official census has been delayed from its scheduled April 2010 date and the results are unlikely to become available before 2013 at the earliest. Expats make up more than 80% of the population with nearly 75% of expat residents hailing from the Asian subcontinent.

Whereas 20 years ago, oil revenues accounted for around half of Dubai's GDP, the oil sector now contributes just a few percentage points. Today, trade, manufacturing, transport, construction and real estate, finance and tourism are the main contributors.

Tourism

The development of high-end hotels and much-publicised visitor attractions – in conjunction with a successful overseas marketing campaign – has made Dubai a popular holiday destination for tourists. Visitors from Britain, India, Iran, Saudi Arabia and the US are the most numerous, with almost one million Brits alone arriving in the emirate each year; in total, Dubai's hotels and hotel apartments welcome nearly 10 million visitors a year.

New Developments

In the wake of the global economic slow-down, some projects have fallen behind their original schedules and others have been put on hold. But several high-profile projects have been completed and work on others is going ahead. The Palm Jumeirah and the Burj Khalifa are among the best examples of fully finalised developments that have come to symbolise Dubai. The city's traffic jams have eased following the completion of the Dubai Metro and work on a separate tramline is underway.

Visiting Dubai

Getting There

Dubai International Airport (DXB) is an important global travel hub, handling more than 50 million passengers in a year. Currently, more than 150 airlines use the airport, flying to over 220 destinations. Terminal 1 handles major international airlines; Terminal 3 is exclusively used by Dubai's Emirates; while Terminal 2 is home to budget

operator flydubai and other lowcost carriers, as well as charter flights. The airport is clean and modern, facilities are good, and there's a huge duty free section in Terminals 1 and 3.

Airport Transfer

If you booked your break through a hotel or travel agency, it's likely that pick-up from the airport will be included. If not, the Metro connects the airport to destinations the length of Dubai directly from Terminals 1 and 3, or you can easily grab a cab. Taxis leaving from the airport charge an extra Dhs.25 so it costs around Dhs.50 for a journey to the hotels of Sheikh Zayed Road and the Downtown area or up to Dhs.90 to Dubai Marina and JBR. An airport bus runs to and from the airport every 30 minutes, 24 hours a day. There are a number of loop routes: C1 runs to Satwa, while the C2 goes to Zabeel Park. See wojhati.rta.ae to plan your journey.

Visas & Customs

Requirements vary depending on your country of origin and it's wise to check the regulations before departure. GCC nationals (Bahrain, Kuwait, Qatar, Oman and Saudi Arabia) do not need a visa to enter Dubai. Citizens from many other countries get an automatic 60 day visa upon arrival at the airport.

Certain medications, including codeine, Temazepam and Prozac, are banned even though they are freely available in other countries. High-profile cases have highlighted the UAE's zero tolerance to drugs. Even a miniscule quantity in your possession could result in a lengthy jail term.

Local Knowledge

Climate

Dubai has a subtropical and arid climate. Sunny blue skies and high temperatures can be expected most of the year. Rainfall is infrequent, averaging only 25 days per year, mainly in winter (December to March). Summer temperatures can hit a soaring 48°C (118°F) and with humidity well above 60% it can make for uncomfortable conditions from June to September. The most pleasant time to visit Dubai is during the winter months when average temperatures range between 14°C and 30°C.

Time

The UAE is four hours ahead of UTC (Universal Coordinated Time – formerly known as GMT). There is no altering of clocks for daylight saving in the summer. Most offices and schools are closed during the weekend, on Fridays and Saturdays. Be aware that the Metro and some shops don't open until later on Fridays.

Electricity & Water

The electricity supply is 220/240 volts and 50 cycles. Most hotel rooms and villas use the three-pin plug that is used in the UK. Adaptors are widely available and only cost a few dirhams. Tap water is desalinated sea water and is perfectly safe to drink although most people choose mineral water because it tastes better and is cheap.

Money

Credit and debit cards are widely accepted around Dubai. Foreign currencies and travellers' cheques can be exchanged in licensed exchange offices, banks and hotels. Cash is preferred in the souks, markets and in smaller shops, and paying in cash will help your bargaining power. If you've hired a car, be aware that only cash is accepted at petrol pumps.

The monetary unit is the dirham (Dhs.), which is divided into 100 fils. The currency is also referred to as AED (Arab Emirate dirham). Notes come in denominations of Dhs.5 (brown), Dhs.10 (green), Dhs.20 (light blue), Dhs.50 (purple), Dhs.100 (pink), Dhs.200 (yellow-brown), Dhs.500 (blue) and Dhs.1,000 (browny-purple). The dirham has been pegged to the US dollar since 1980, at a mid rate of $1 to Dhs.3.6725.

Language

Arabic is the official language of the UAE, although English, Hindi, Malayalam and Urdu are commonly spoken. You can easily get by with English, but you're likely to receive at least a smile if you can throw in a couple of Arabic words.

Crime & Safety

Pickpocketing and crimes against tourists are a rarity in Dubai, and visitors can enjoy feeling safe and unthreatened in most places around town. Dubai Police will advise you on a course of action in the case of a loss or theft. If you've lost something in a taxi, call the taxi company. If you lose your passport, your next stop should be your embassy or consulate. With high accident rates, extra caution should be taken on Dubai's roads, whether navigating the streets on foot or in a vehicle. There is zero tolerance towards drink driving, even after one pint, and if you're caught you can expect a spell in prison.

Accidents & Emergencies

If you witness an accident or need an ambulance in an emergency situation, the number to call is 999. For urgent medical care, there are several private hospitals with excellent A&E facilities. Anyone can receive emergency treatment in government hospitals but note that charges apply to those without Dubai health cards. For general non-emergency medical care, most hospitals have a walk-in clinic where you can simply turn up.

People With Disabilities

Dubai is starting to consider the needs of visitors with special needs more seriously although, in general, facilities remain somewhat limited, particularly at older attractions. Dubai International Airport is well equipped for visitors with special needs thanks to automatic doors and large lifts, as well as services such as porters, special transportation and wheelchair accessible check-in counters. All Metro stations have both easy access to wheelchair users and tactile floor routes for visually impaired people. Most of the newer malls also have wheelchair access, while five-star and recently built hotels offer accessible rooms for visitors with special needs.

Telephone & Internet

It is possible to buy temporary (three month) SIM cards for mobile phones that work on a pay-as-you go basis. Etisalat's 'Ahlan' package costs Dhs.60, including Dhs.25 credit and lasting 90 days. du's pre-paid package costs Dhs.55 with a welcome bonus of Dhs.10, usage bonus of Dhs.100, and lifetime validity (provided minimum top-ups are made). You can easily buy top-up cards for both packages from supermarkets, newsagents and petrol stations. WiFi is available in many hotels and cafes around town.

Media & Further Reading

Many of the major glossy magazines are available in Dubai, but if they're imported from the US or Europe, you can expect to pay at least twice the normal cover price. Alternatively, you can pick up the Middle East versions of popular titles including *Harper's Bazaar*, *Grazia*, *OK!* and *Hello!* where you'll find all the regular gossip and news, with extras from around the region. All international titles are examined and, where necessary, censored to ensure that they don't offend the country's moral codes.

Television

Most hotels have satellite or cable, broadcasting a mix of local and international channels. You'll find MTV, major news stations and some BBC programming, in addition to the standard hotel info loop. For a slice of local flavour, check out local stations City7, Dubai TV and Dubai One.

Radio

Catering for Dubai's multinational inhabitants, there are stations broadcasting in English, French, Hindi, Malayalam and Urdu. Of the English speaking stations, there is a good range to choose from. Tune into Dubai 92 (92.0 FM), Radio 1 (104.1 FM), Radio 2 (99.3 FM), The Coast (103.2) and Virgin Radio (104.4 FM) for music or Dubai Eye (103.8 FM) for talk radio and sport. You can pick up BBC World Service on 87.9 FM.

Public Holidays & Annual Events

Public Holidays

The Islamic calendar starts from the year 622AD, the year of Prophet Muhammad's migration (Hijra) from Mecca to Al Madinah. Hence, the Islamic year is called the Hijri year and dates are followed by AH (AH stands for Anno Hegirae, meaning 'after the year of the Hijra'). As some holidays are based on the sighting of the moon and do not have fixed dates on the Hijri calendar, Islamic holidays are more often than not confirmed less than 24 hours in advance. The main Muslim festivals are Eid Al Fitr (the festival of the breaking of the fast, which marks the end of Ramadan) and Eid Al Adha (the festival of the sacrifice, which marks the end of the pilgrimage to Mecca). Mawlid Al Nabee is the holiday celebrating Prophet Muhammad's birthday, and Lailat Al Mi'raj celebrates the Prophet's ascension into heaven.

In general, public holidays are unlikely to disrupt a visit to Dubai, except that shops may open a bit later and, on a few specific days, alcohol is not served. During Ramadan, food and beverages cannot be consumed in public during the day; however, in most tourist hotels, there are special areas which serve diners all day long.

Annual Events

Dubai hosts an impressive array of events, from the world's richest horse race and international tennis to well-respected jazz and film festivals. Many attract thousands of visitors and tickets often sell out quickly.

Dubai Shopping Festival

January to February
dubaievents.ae
Bargains galore for shoppers.

Omega Dubai Desert Classic

February
dubaidesertclassic.com
Longstanding PGA European Tour fixture popular among Dubai's golfing community.

Dubai is the regional hub for major international events, which range from trade exhibitions to cultural fairs. But the most highly-anticipated are the main annual sporting events, such as the Dubai Rugby Sevens and the Dubai World Cup, both of which are as much about partying as they are about sport.

Dubai Duty Free Tennis Championships

March

dubaidutyfreetennis
championships.com

Attracts the world's top men's and women's seeds.

Dubai World Cup

March

dubaiworldcup.com

The richest horse race in the world.

Camel Racing

October to April

Popular local sport that is serious business. Races take place during winter from 07:00 to 08:30.

Dubai World Championship

November

dubaiworldchampionship.com

The final fixture of the Race To Dubai tournament in which the world's best have a shot at a share of the $7.5 million prize fund.

Skywards Dubai International Jazz Festival

December

dubaijazzfest.com

Attracts a broad range of artists from all around the world.

Dubai International Film Festival

December

dubaifilmfest.com

Showcase of Hollywood, international and regional films.

Emirates Airlines Dubai Rugby Sevens

December

dubairugby7s.com

Over 130,000 people come to watch top teams and party until the wee hours.

Getting Around

Metro

The Red Line runs from Rashidiya and the airport down Sheikh Zayed Road – passing the financial district, Downtown, Al Barsha and Dubai Marina – before terminating at Jebel Ali. The Green Line runs from Al Qusais on the Sharjah border to Jaddaf. Trains run from around 06:00 to 24:00 on weekdays, and until 01:00 during the weekend; on Fridays, the service starts at 13:00. Each train has a section for women and children only, and a first class cabin. The metro is a fantastic way to do some sightseeing: the majority of the route is above ground, meaning you'll get a bird's eye view of the city from one end to the other. A separate monorail runs the length of Palm Jumeirah to Atlantis. Trains run from 08:00 to 22:00 and cost Dhs.15 for a single fare or Dhs.25 for a return.

Bus

There are dozens of bus routes servicing the main residential and commercial areas of Dubai. The buses and bus shelters are air-conditioned, modern and clean, although they can be rather crowded at peak times. Buses run at regular intervals until around midnight and a handful of Nightliner buses operate from 23:30 till 06:00. The front three rows of seats on all buses are reserved for women and children only. You need to purchase a Nol card before boarding as cash is not accepted.

Driving & Car Hire

Drivers are erratic, roads are constantly changing and the traffic jams can be enduring. On the bright side, most cars are automatic, which makes city driving a lot easier. If you are a confident driver, you'll probably find that driving in Dubai looks much worse than it is in practice. Expect the unexpected and use your mirrors and indicators. International car rental companies, plus a few local firms, can be found in Dubai. Prices range from Dhs.80 a day for smaller cars to Dhs.1,000 for limousines. Comprehensive insurance is essential; make sure that it includes personal accident coverage. To rent a car, you are required to produce a copy of your passport, a valid international driving licence and a credit card. Parking is plentiful at most malls and is free for at least the first three hours. Street parking spaces can be hard to find but cost just Dhs.2 for one hour.

Nol cards are the convenient, rechargeable travel cards used to pay for public transport. The red Nol is a paper ticket aimed at tourists and occasional users, while the silver Nol is better if you plan to travel extensively while in town. You can buy Nol cards from Metro stations and the larger supermarkets.

Taxi

Taxis remain the common way of getting around, especially among tourists. There are seven companies operating nearly 8,000 metered cabs in the city, with a common fixed fare structure. All cars are clean and modern, and the fares are cheaper than in most international cities. A fleet of 'ladies' taxis', with distinctive pink roofs and female drivers, are meant for female passengers and families only.

The minimum fare is currently Dhs.10 although the pickup charge from the airport is Dhs.25. It is also possible to hire a taxi for 12 or 24 hour periods. Taxis can be flagged down by the side of the road, or you can order one through Dubai Transport by calling 04 208 0808. This number is also useful for complaints and lost item inquiries, both of which are usually dealt with promptly.

Walking

Most cities in the UAE are very car-oriented and not designed to encourage walking. Additionally, summer temperatures of more than 45°C are not conducive to a leisurely stroll. The winter months, however, make walking a pleasant way to explore. There aren't many pavements in Dubai, however Downtown Dubai and Dubai Marina are attractive communities designed with pedestrians in mind. Both are interesting places to walk around with plenty of cafes and shops to tempt you off the street.

Water Bus

Crossing the creek by a traditional abra is a common method of transport for many people living in Bur Dubai and Deira; for visitors, it's a must-do experience while in town. Abra stations have been upgraded recently, but the fares are still just Dhs.1.

Another recent addition to the creek is a fleet of air-conditioned water buses. These operate on four different routes crossing the creek, with fares set at Dhs.2 per one way trip. A 'tourist' route also operates, with a 45 minute creek tour costing around Dhs.25 per person.

It's also possible to take a scenic cruise on RTA's new Dubai Ferry; the modern ferries whisk you on a scenic ride and the routes depart from Dubai Marina and Al Seef (rta.ae).

Places To Stay

In addition to a high number of plush hotels, Dubai has plenty of four, three, two and one-star places, self-catering villas, hotel apartments and even a youth hostel. The coastal options will probably allow access to a private beach, but if you're in Dubai on business then proximity to the financial and business areas of DIFC and Trade Centre is likely to be a priority. If you're here for a few days, why not combine your city stay with a night at a desert resort, such as Bab Al Shams (p.78)? The most popular hotels tend to get fully booked up in the high season, but big discounts and attractive packages are often on offer for those visiting during the summer months.

The Address Downtown Dubai
theaddress.com
04 436 8888
Map p.216
Metro Burj Khalifa/Dubai Mall

Armani Hotel Dubai
dubai.armanihotels.com
04 888 3888
Map p.216
Metro Burj Khalifa/Dubai Mall

Atlantis The Palm
atlantisthepalm.com
04 426 0000
Map Overview Map **Metro** Nakheel

Bonnington Jumeirah Lakes Towers
bonningtontower.com
04 356 0000
Map p.211
Metro Jumeirah Lakes Towers

Burj Al Arab
jumeirah.com
04 301 7777
Map p.213 **Metro** Mall Of The Emirates

Dubai Festival City
ichotelsgroup.com
Map p.223 **Metro** Emirates

Grosvenor House
grosvenorhouse.lemeridien.com
04 399 8888
Map p.211 **Metro** Dubai Marina

Hilton Dubai Jumeirah Resort
hilton.com
04 399 1111
Map p.211 **Metro** Dubai Marina

Jumeirah Beach Hotel
jumeirah.com
04 348 0000
Map p.213 **Metro** Mall Of The Emirates

Le Royal Meridien Beach Resort & Spa
leroyalmeridien-dubai.com
04 399 5555
Map p.211 **Metro** Dubai Marina

Madinat Jumeirah
jumeirah.com
04 366 8888
Map p.213 **Metro** Mall Of The Emirates

One&Only Royal Mirage
oneandonlyresorts.com
04 399 9999
Map p.212 **Metro** Nakheel

The Palace – The Old Town
theaddress.com
04 428 7888
Map p.216
Metro Burj Khalifa/Dubai Mall

Park Hyatt Dubai
dubai.park.hyatt.com
04 602 1234
Map p.218 **Metro** GGICO

Raffles Dubai
raffles.com
04 324 8888
Map p.218 **Metro** Healthcare City

The Ritz-Carlton, Dubai
ritzcarlton.com
04 399 4000
Map p.211 **Metro** Dubai Marina

Sofitel Dubai Jumeirah Beach
sofitel.com
04 448 4848
Map p.211 **Metro** Jumeirah Lakes Towers

The Westin Dubai Mina Seyahi Beach Resort & Marina
westinminaseyahi.com
04 399 4141
Map p.211 **Metro** Nakheel

Unlike in much of the rest of the world, where hotels provide accommodation and meeting rooms, much of Dubai's social scene revolves around its hotels, as they're where you'll usually find the best restaurants, bars, beach bars and clubs.

Explore Authentic Emirati Culture

Open doors. Open minds.

Sheikh Mohammed
Centre for Cultural Understanding

الأبواب مفتوحة. العقول منفتحة.

مركز الشيخ محمد بن راشد آل مكتوم
للتواصل الحضاري

tel: 9714 353 6666
www.cultures.ae

Cultural Attractions

Bastakiya & Dubai Museum	16
Jumeirah Mosque	18
Art Galleries	19
Abra Crossing	22
Camel Racing	23
Heritage Village	24
Fish Market	25
Majlis Ghorfat Um Al Sheif	26
Falcon & Heritage Sports Centre	27
Sheikh Mohammed Centre For Cultural Understanding	29

Cultural
Attractions
Introduction

The emirate of Dubai features many fascinating places to visit, offering glimpses into a time when the city was nothing more than a small fishing and trading port.

Dubai manages what some Arab cities fail to achieve: a healthy balance between western influences and eastern traditions. Its culture is very much rooted in the Islamic customs that deeply penetrate the Arabian Peninsula and beyond.

However, the UAE's successful effort to become modern and cosmopolitan is proof of an open-minded and liberal outlook. Consequently, the rapid economic development over the last 30 years has changed life in the emirates beyond recognition.

Yet the country's rulers are committed to safeguarding their heritage, and have gone to huge lengths to promote cultural and sporting events that are representative of the region's traditions. Falconry, camel racing and traditional dhow sailing are all popular, as is Arabic poetry, dancing, songs and traditional art and craftsmanship. Courtesy and hospitality are the most highly prized virtues, and visitors are likely to experience the genuine warmth and friendliness of the Emirati people during their stay.

Old Dubai features many fascinating places to visit, offering glimpses into a time when the city was nothing more than a small fishing and trading port. Many of the pre-oil heritage sites have been carefully restored, paying close attention to traditional design and using original building materials. Stroll through the Bastakiya area, with its many distinctive windtowers, and marvel at how people coped in Dubai before air-conditioning. Dubai Museum and Jumeirah Mosque both offer interesting insights into local culture. While there's nothing like the Tate or the Louvre in Dubai yet, there are a number of galleries that have interesting exhibitions of art and traditional Arabic artefacts, and more are springing up, particularly in the Al Quoz area (p.19). Meanwhile, the Dubai Modern Art Museum and Opera House District are currently being constructed in Downtown Dubai, off the Burj Lake, so look out for those in the future.

Ramadan Timings

During the Islamic holy month of Ramadan, Muslims fast from sunrise to sunset for 30 days. The exact dates of Ramadan change every year due to the fact that Islam uses a lunar calendar (each month begins with the sighting of a new moon). As a result, Islamic holidays begin on different days each year with Ramadan taking place 11 days earlier each year according to the western Gregorian calendar. It is worth checking when you will be visiting Dubai as, during Ramadan, timings for many companies change significantly. Museums and heritage sites, for instance, usually open slightly later in the morning than usual, and close earlier in the afternoon.

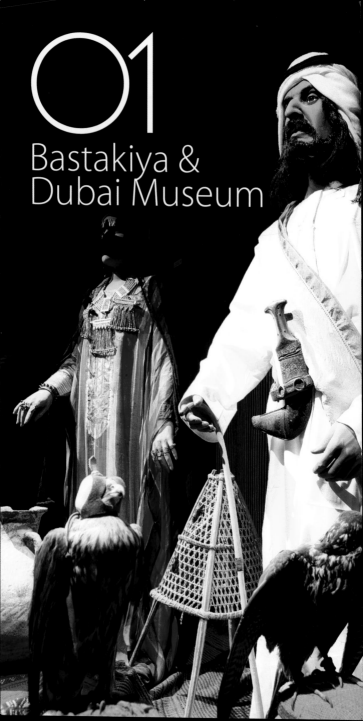

O1
Bastakiya &
Dubai Museum

Location Al Souk Al Kabeer **Web** definitelydubai.com
Tel 04 353 1862 **Times** 08:30-20:30 (daily),14:30-20:30 (Friday)
Price Guide Dhs.3 (adults), Dhs.1 (children) **Map** **1** p.218

For a dose of tradition, step out of the modern world and into a small pocket of the city that harks back to a bygone era. Located in Bur Dubai next to Dubai Creek, the Bastakiya district is one of the oldest heritage sites in the city. The neighbourhood dates from the early 1900s, when traders from the Bastak area of southern Iran were encouraged to settle there by tax concessions granted by Sheikh Maktoum Bin Hashar, the ruler of Dubai at the time. Today, Bastakiya is among Dubai's most atmospheric areas to explore thanks to its traditional windtower houses which are built around courtyards and clustered together along a winding maze of alleyways. The distinctive four-sided windtowers (barjeel), seen on top of the traditional flat-roofed buildings, were an early form of air conditioning, capturing the breeze and channelling it down into the houses. Some excellent cultural establishments, including the Dubai Museum and various art galleries, are also here, while a short stroll along the creek will bring you to the Textile Souk and an abra station from where you can cross the water to explore the souks on the Deira side of Dubai.

Dubai Museum

Located in Al Fahidi Fort, this museum is interesting for all the family. The fort was originally built in 1787 as the residence of the ruler of Dubai and for sea defence, and then renovated in 1970 to house the museum. All aspects of Dubai's past are represented; you can walk through a souk from the 1950s, stroll through an oasis, see into a traditional house, get up close to local wildlife, learn about the archaeological finds or go 'underwater' to discover pearl diving and fishing. There are some entertaining mannequins to pose with, too.

The Sheikh Mohammed Centre for Cultural Understanding (p.29) offers a number of walking tours around Bastakiya's heritage sites – well worth attending.

Jumeirah Mosque

Location Jumeira 1 **Web** cultures.ae
Tel 04 353 6666 **Times** tour starts at 10:00 (Saturday, Sunday, Tuesday & Thursday) **Price Guide** Dhs.10 **Map** 2 p.217

This is the most beautiful mosque in the city and perhaps the best known, as its image features on the Dhs.500 banknote. The Sheikh Mohammed Centre for Cultural Understanding (p.29) organises tours for non-Muslims, with visitors being guided around the mosque, before the hosts offer a talk on Islam and explain prayer rituals. The tour is a fascinating insight into the culture and beliefs of the local population, and is thoroughly recommended. You must dress conservatively – no shorts or sleeveless tops, and skirts must be below the knee. Additionally, women must cover their hair with a head scarf, and all visitors will be asked to remove their shoes.

03
Art Galleries

Location various **Web** artdubai.ae
Times 10:00-22:00 (daily, closed Friday)
Price Guide Free

Dubai is one of major Arab
destinations for art lovers. Thanks
to its location, the emirate offers
the perfect mix of Western, Asian
and Middle Eastern art. Most art
houses operate as a shop and
and a gallery, while others also
provide studios for artists. The Majlis
Gallery (themajlisgallery.com) and
the XVA Gallery (xvagallery.com)
in Bastakiya are worth visiting for
their architecture alone, while at
Opera Gallery (operagallery.com) in
DIFC, you'll find the odd Renoir and
Picasso. To discover Dubai's real art
scene, however, there's no better area
than the emirate's best kept secret:
Al Quoz. Tucked away in massive
warehouses – often out of sight – are
a collection of galleries featuring
local and international art, as well
as a number of impressive interior
design shops. It is here that lesser-
known artists can find exhibition
space. If you've the patience to
explore, you will be rewarded with
the quality on display.

Galleries to look out for in Al
Quoz include 4 Walls Art Gallery,
The Third Line, Ayyam Gallery,
The Mojo Gallery, Carbon12 and
Gallery Isabelle Van Den Eynde.
For up-to-date listings on
upcoming exhibitions, visit
askexplorer.com.

Part of what is now known as 'old Dubai', the Creek is an incredibly atmospheric area, featuring beautiful scenery, narrow streets bustling with activity, and traders hauling their cargo off and on to the interestingly decorated dhows.

For the full Dubai Creek experience, visitors can head to the Textile Souk on the Bur Dubai side before taking a trip across the water to Deira on a commuter abra.

04

Abra Crossing

Location Deira & Bur Dubai **Times** 05:00-00:00 (daily)
Price Guide Dhs.1 **Map** 4 p.218

Once the central residential hub of
Dubai, Deira remains an incredibly
atmospheric area. Narrow, convoluted
streets bustle with activity while gold,
spices, perfumes and general goods
are touted in its numerous souks.
Likewise, Dubai Creek – beside which
Deira sits – was the original centre of
the emirate's commerce, and it still
buzzes today with boats zipping up
and down, plying their transport and
cargo trades. No visitor should miss
the chance to experience a trip across
the water on a commuter abra for the
bargain price of Dhs.1. Alternatively,
you can actually hire your own abra
(plus driver) for an hour-long creek

tour for Dhs.100. For the full creek
experience, start at Bastakiya, before
wandering through the Textile Souk
on the Bur Dubai side, then take an
abra towards Deira. Once on the Deira
side, cross the corniche and head
towards the souk district. First stop is
the Spice Souk, where the aroma of
saffron and cumin fills the air. Nearby,
the streets in and around the Gold
Souk are crammed with shops
shimmering with gold, silver and
platinum. Finally, take a wander
around the area behind the souks to
discover alleyways and narrow streets
with shops that deal in almost any
kind of goods imaginable.

05

Camel Racing

Location various
Times 07:30 (Thursday & Friday)
Price Guide free **Map** 5 p.209

This is a chance to see a truly traditional and unique local sport close up. Races take place during the winter months at tracks across the UAE. Every tour operator in the emirate is familiar with the location of Dubai's race track (by the Al Lisali exit on Al Ain road past Dubai Outlet Mall). However, it is recommended that you visit as part of a group. Outside of the emirate, Ras Al Khaimah has one of the best racetracks in the country at Digdagga, situated on a plain between the dunes and the mountains. Apart from great photo opportunities and the excitement of the races, you can also have a browse around the stalls; most race tracks have camel markets alongside. The best buys are the large cotton blankets (used as camel blankets), which double up as excellent bedspreads and throws, and only cost around Dhs.40.

Racing camels used to be ridden by children, but this practice has been outlawed – and robotic jockeys have taken over. The operators follow the race in 4WDs while directing the jockeys by remote control – quite a bizarre sight.

Heritage Village

Location Al Shindagha **Web** definitelydubai.com
Tel 04 393 9913 **Times** 08:30-22:00 (Saturday to Thursday),
15:30-22:00 (Friday)
Price Guide free **Map** 6 p.218

Located near the entrance
to Dubai Creek, the
Heritage Village focuses
on Dubai's maritime past,
pearl diving traditions and
architecture. Visitors can
observe traditional potters
and weavers practising their
crafts the way they have
for centuries. Local women
serve traditionally cooked
snacks – one of the
rare opportunities you'll have
to sample genuine Emirati
cuisine. The village is very
close to Sheikh Saeed Al
Maktoum's House, the home
of the much-loved former
ruler of Dubai.

Fish Market

Location Corniche Deira
Times from 04:30 (daily)
Map 7 p.219

The Fish Market in Deira is hard to ignore if you're in the area – maybe not the best place to visit if you don't like the smell of fish. To experience the vibrancy of this working market, head down early in the morning or late at night as the catch is coming in off the boats. You can purchase fresh fish here, but do get involved in some haggling. For an additional fee, your fish can be cleaned and gutted before being taken to the market's restaurant where the catch is grilled or fried to your liking. Side dishes such as rice and salad are also available to complete your meal.

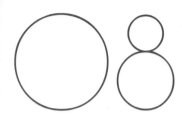

Majlis Ghorfat Um Al Sheif

Location Jumeira 3 **Web** definitelydubai.com
Tel 04 852 1374 **Times** 08:30-20:30 (Saturday to Thursday),
14:30-20:30 (Friday)
Price Guide Dhs.1 **Map** 8 p.215

Constructed in 1955 from coral stone and gypsum, Majlis Ghorfat Um Al Sheif was used by the late Sheikh Rashid Bin Saeed Al Maktoum as a summer residence. The ground floor of the simple building features an open veranda (known as a *leewan* or *rewaaq*), while, upstairs, the *majlis* (the Arabic term for meeting place) is decorated with carpets, cushions, lanterns and rifles. The roof terrace was used for drying dates and even sleeping on and it originally offered an uninterrupted view of the sea, although all you can see now are rooftops. The site has a garden with a pond, a traditional *falaj* irrigation system and a palm leaf barasti shelter.

Majlis Ghorfat Um Al Sheif receives around 200 visitors from different nationalities every day. The building is also a popular dining spot for Emirati picnickers.

09

Falcon & Heritage Sports Centre

Location Meydan **Web** dm.gov.ae
Tel 800 900 **Times** 09:00-22:00 (daily except Friday)
Price Guide free **Map** 9 p.209

Falconry has been practised in the UAE for centuries, and it continues to play an integral part of desert life. So it comes as no surprise that the falcon is the national bird of the Emirates. In the past, these powerful and fast birds were trained and used by Bedouin tribes as hunters; nowadays, falconry continues to be practised but as a sport. It is still considered a very popular, traditional Emirati pastime. Nad Al Sheba's National Falcon and Heritage Sports Centre houses a number of birds of prey, which are available for sale to traders – the only place in Dubai where birds of prey can be legally sold. There's also a mini museum dedicated to falcons, plus a souk where accessories, such as protective gauntlets, bird hoods, and even horse-riding equipment are all sold.

10

Sheikh Mohammed Centre For Cultural Understanding

Location Bastakiya, Al Souk Al Kabeer **Web** cultures.ae
Tel 04 353 6666 **Times** 08:00-15:00 (Sunday to Thursday),
09:00-13:00 (Saturday)
Price Guide Dhs.10 to Dhs.70 **Map** 10 p.218

Located in the Bastakiya area of the city, The Sheikh Mohammed Centre for Cultural Understanding (SMCCU) is a non-profit organisation that was established to help visitors and residents understand the customs and traditions of the UAE through various activities and outings. Operating under the slogan 'Open Doors, Open Minds' the centre focuses on removing barriers between different nationalities, and raising awareness of the local culture, customs and religion of the UAE. Programmes include fascinating guided tours of Jumeirah Mosque (Dhs.10), walking tours around Bastakiya's heritage sites (Dhs.35 for 60 minutes), cultural awareness sessions (Dhs.25) and coffee mornings (Dhs.60) where UAE nationals explain their way of life. The building that houses the centre is also worth a look for the majlis-style rooms located around the courtyard and great views through the palm trees and windtowers.

During Ramadan, the SMCCU hosts daily iftars, where you can break fast in a traditional setting. Tickets cost Dhs.135 and include a three-course Emirati meal and Bastakiya tour. This event is popular so book online in advance.

BECOME A LEGEND

MASTER THE ART OF INDOOR SKYDIVING

Defy gravity with skill, style and courage at iFLY Dubai !

Get your adrenaline fix at the Region's only indoor skydiving venue, complete with expert trainers, climate control and state-of-the-art technology. Sharpen your skills or ride the wind for the very first time in a fun-filled challenge that's enjoyable for kids as young as 5 and a great day out for the entire family.

Log on to www.facebook.com/playnationme to find out more.

iFLY DUBAI

playnation

LEVEL 1, MIRDIF CITY CENTRE

Family
Fun

Dubai Aquarium

Family Fun
Introduction

A large part of Dubai's appeal is that it truly is a destination that has something for everyone, with some stunning attractions that cater for the whole family.

Family is a huge part of life in Dubai, as well as an integral part of Emirati culture, and no matter where you go, children are rarely expected to be seen and not heard in Dubai. Many restaurants are abuzz with kids running around and there are numerous weekend brunches aimed specifically at families, with entertainment such as face painting, bouncy castles, art classes and games all laid on to help the younger family members enjoy the day every bit as much as mum and dad.

As well as some of the more individual family attractions listed in this chapter, the giant malls of Dubai provide bounteous destinations when it comes to keeping kids entertained. While some boast facilities that are giant attractions in their own right – like Ski Dubai (p.144), KidZania, Sega Republic (p.44) and Playnation (p.38) – almost all malls have some sort of entertainment centre or games areas. Cinemas also have a pretty open door policy, although you'd do well to respect the recommended age restrictions, as much out of consideration for other patrons as well as the enjoyment for your children.

During the cooler months, Dubai's parks are great family locations, and you'll find everything from children's play areas with climbing frames, swings and slides to kiosks renting out bikes and pedal-powered go-karts at the majority of parks now. And an ice cream stand or two to boot, of course.

If you're staying at one of Dubai's bigger resorts, the children may not ever want to leave the hotel, such are

the range of activities available, from kids' clubs to swimming pools, and beaches to watersports. Some resorts, such as Jumeirah Beach Hotel, even offer kids' fitness classes, sporting tournaments and coaching, as well as specialist facilities, like a climbing wall.

If your hotel doesn't have a pool, then, other than the amazing waterparks, the beach is really the only option as public pools outside of hotels and sports clubs are rare in Dubai. You can find public pools at Mushrif Park (men and women have separate pools here), although a better option may be to get a day pass at one of the bigger resort hotels, giving you access to the pool and facilities for a full day. Some of the resorts offer watersports and many of these aquatic thrills, including donutting and banana boat riding, are also suitable activities for teens. A word of caution while out and about by the beach, however: unless your child is a particularly strong swimmer, it is unwise to let them swim in the sea unsupervised, especially at the public beaches, as there can sometimes be strong undercurrents.

Choosing hotels

Check out what activities come included with your hotel booking before making a reservation. Hotels like Atlantis, The Palm, for example, may be at the pricier end of the spectrum but if you factor in the free entry to Aquaventure (p.45) and The Lost Chambers, it can become an attractive option – especially for families with several kids.

01
Wild Wadi

Location Umm Suqeim 3
Web wildwadi.com
Tel 04 348 4444
Times 10:00-20:00 (daily)
Price Guide Dhs.145-Dhs.220
Map 1 p.213

Spread out over 12 acres between Jumeirah Beach Hotel and Jumeirah Madinat (p.10), Wild Wadi is one of the world's best waterparks, with a host of aquatic rides and attractions to suit all ages and bravery levels. Depending on how busy it is, you may have to queue for some of the rides, but it's worth the wait – especially as, once you're on the main Master Blaster ride, it's effectively 12 rides in one, as you choose which slide to power down in your inflatable tube before powerful jets blast you back uphill to try another. Other highlights include the Wipeout and Riptide flowriders (permanently rolling waves that are ideal for perfecting your body-boarding skills), and the four-seater rides Burj Surj and Tantrum Alley – not to mention the thrilling, newly improved Jumeirah Sceirah.

> Anyone staying at a Jumeirah hotel gets complimentary access to Wild Wadi, as well as a free buggy or shuttle service – worth considering when making you booking.

O2
KidZania

Location The Dubai Mall **Web** kidzania.ae **Tel** 04 448 5222
Times 09:00-22:00 (Sunday to Wednesday), 09:00-00:00 (Thursday), 10:00-00:00 (Friday & Saturday) **Price Guide** Dhs.90-Dhs.130 **Map 2** p.216

Billed as a 'real-life city' for children, KidZania is a fantastic attraction and is enough to make even the most grown-up of adults wish that they were 10 years old again. Essentially, KidZania is a fantasy world where kids can dress up and act out more than 75 real world roles, from policeman to pilot, doctor to designer. The KidZania city even has its own currency, Kidzos, which children can earn by performing certain roles and services, and spend on food or activities. It's a clever combination of entertainment and local businesses: for example, upon arrival into KidZania, children need to go and open an account at HSBC in order to obtain Kidzos. They can earn money

working at the likes of Sony, Jotun or Swatch, or even 'study' to become a firefighter or doctor. The latest jobs to be added include becoming an installation engineer for du, a car sales representative or a comic book artist, baking biscuits at the Britannia Biscuit Factory, or learning how to inspect parcels for Dubai Customs. Once work is done, it's time to spend Kidzos on makeovers, arts and crafts, or at the race track. Or maybe head for McDonalds, Baskin Robbins or Pizza Express for a bite to eat. It's both fun and educational, but also very safe – remote frequency ID bracelets ensure that children can only leave KidZania when the adult with whom they entered is in tow.

Adventure HQ

Location Times Square Center **Web** adventurehq.ae
Tel 04 346 6824 **Times** 10:00-22:00 (Saturday to Wednesday),
10:00-00:00 (Thursday & Friday)
Price Guide Dhs.50-Dhs.125 **Map** **3** p.214

As well as being arguably the best place in the UAE to pick up climbing, hiking and general outdoor gear, Adventure HQ is also an essential stop for a spot of lofty indoor fun. You'll find a state-of-the-art 'climbing pinnacle' – a climbing wall that you can tackle from all sides, which means that there's an incredible number of routes to choose of varying difficulties. For those with military aspirations, there's also the cable climb, which is an adrenaline-spiking assault course that is suspended from the very high ceiling. You can opt to try either activity separately or get a multi-pass if you think you're brave enough to tackle both.

The northern emirates of the UAE offer some exceptional climbing terrain but, back in Dubai, there are also walls open to the public at World Trade Centre (climbingdubai.com) and at Pharaohs' Club (wafi.com).

O4
Snow Park

Location Ski Dubai **Web** theplaymania.com
Tel 800 386 **Times** 10:00-23:00 (Sunday to Wednesday),
10:00-00:00 (Thursday), 09:00-00:00 (Friday), 09:00-11:00 (Saturday)
Price Guide Dhs.120-Dhs.595 **Map 4** p.213

Part of the Middle East's first indoor ski resort, Ski Dubai, where temperatures hover at around -3 °c, even when it's closer to +50 °c outside, this is the biggest indoor snow park anywhere in the world and, for the little ones who don't want to take to the slopes, or are too young to ski, this is one of the coolest experiences in Dubai. There's a twin track bobsleigh run, an exciting snow cavern, a toboggan run and the potential to upgrade and experience some extra activities, such as zorbing (rolling down the slope in a giant inflatable ball), taking a ride on the chairlift which goes all the way to the top of the black run, or even meeting the penguins who live at Ski Dubai. Snow Park entry includes the hire of jackets, trousers and boots.

If you get a bit chilly while in Ski Dubai, jump on the chairlift and head to the Avalanche Cafe, which is halfway up the main slope and serves up finger-thawing coffees and hot chocolates, as well as soft drinks.

05

iFLY Dubai &
Playnation

Location Mirdif City Centre **Web** theplaymania.com
Tel 04 231 6292 **Times** 10:00-23:00 (Sunday to Wednesday),
10:00-00:00 (Thursday to Saturday)
Price Guide Dhs.195 **Map** **5** p.223

Whether you're practising before
making the big jump for real or this
is as close to skydiving as you ever
get, iFly is a whole lot of fun. Located
in Playnation Mirdif City Centre, the
indoor skydiving centre has giant
vertical wind tunnels that simulate
the sensation of jumping from a
plane, but at a fraction of the cost
and with an instructor on hand to
help you perfect the technique. A fun
experience for kids and adults, it's so
realistic that actual skydivers head to
iFly for the longer 'freefall' time. Once
you're done at iFly, there's plenty more
to do at Playnation, with a range of
other exciting activities (and not all
just for younger family members),
Soccer Circus Dubai (an indoor
sports facility with an academy), Yalla!
Bowling, and Magic Planet (which
includes the nerve-wracking Sky
Trail attraction), while the youngest
family members will enjoy the Little
Explorers edutainment centre. There
are pool and air hockey tables, video
games and simulators too; if you get
through that little lot, it must be time
to hit the cinema next door.

If you want a unique holiday
memento, you can buy
photographs and videos of
your iFly experience – some
of the funny faces that get
pulled in the wind tunnel will
keep you laughing all the
way home.

O6

Dubai Aquarium & Underwater Zoo

Location The Dubai Mall **Web** thedubaiaquarium.com
Tel 04 448 5200 **Times** 10:00-22:00 (Sunday to Wednesday),
10:00-00:00 (Thursday to Saturday)
Price Guide Dhs.290 **Map** 6 p.216

Its location may be a little unusual – in the middle of The Dubai Mall – but that's Dubai for you. And it doesn't subtract from what is a fantastic family day out. The aquarium displays over 33,000 tropical fish – passing shoppers can see these for free but, if you want to get close to the 400 rays and sharks, including the fearsome looking but generally friendly sand tiger sharks, then you can walk through the 270° viewing tunnel that runs through the 51m long aquarium. Also well worth a look is the Underwater Zoo, which is located above the aquarium and is home to residents such as penguins, piranhas and an octopus, all divided into three 'ecological zones'.

If you're feeling really adventurous during your visit to Dubai Aquarium, you can go for a scuba dive in the tank (p.147), take a ride on the glass-bottomed boat or even feed the sharks.

Dubai Ice Rink

Location The Dubai Mall **Web** dubaiicerink.com
Tel 04 448 5111 **Times** 10:00-22:00pm (Sunday to Wednesday),
11:15-00:00 (Thursday & Friday)
Price Guide Dhs.55 **Map** 7 p.216

If you want to escape the heat and take to the ice, you've a few options in Dubai, and you'll find skating rinks at both Al Nasr Leisureland (alnasrll. com) and the Hyatt Regency hotel (dubai.regency.hyatt.com). However, the newest and arguably best place to strap on your skates is here at The Dubai Mall, where you'll find this Olympic-size arena overlooked by restaurants, cafes and shops. There are plenty of public skating sessions throughout the day, with daily 'snow babies' and 'moms and tots' sessions also a daily occurrence. Mondays, Thursdays, Fridays and Saturdays are special disco nights but, if you're more Bambi on ice than Torvill and Dean, there are both individual and group classes available daily too. 'Penguin pals' are a good option for youngsters – these gliding skating aids help little ones to stay upright as they learn to skate.

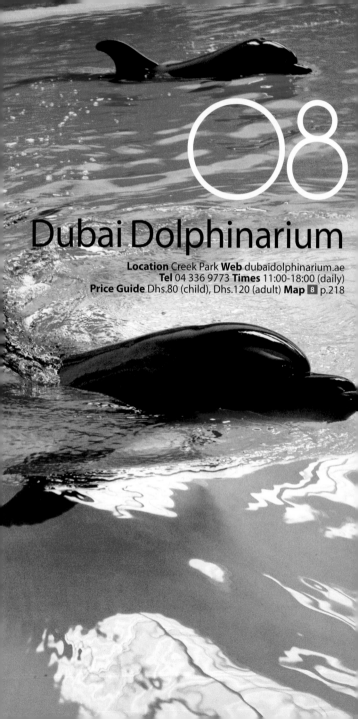

08

Dubai Dolphinarium

Location Creek Park **Web** dubaidolphinarium.ae
Tel 04 336 9773 **Times** 11:00-18:00 (daily)
Price Guide Dhs.80 (child), Dhs.120 (adult) **Map** 8 p.218

Part of the Creekside Park, which has a number of attractions to keep the family busy for an afternoon, the Dolphinarium has proven to be a popular addition since it opened in 2008; being fully indoor and air-conditioned, it's also an attraction that can be enjoyed year-round. The main attraction here is the seal and dolphin show, which runs twice a day during the week, and three times daily at weekends when there's a real carnival atmosphere, thanks to the mascots, clowns, jugglers and puppet shows. Shows last around 45 minutes and, during the dolphin show, you will get to meet the three resident black sea bottlenose dolphins and the four northern fur seals. The way that both dolphins and seals react and interact with their trainers brings a smile to the face while showing just how intelligent both of these magnificent creatures are. Afterwards, you can have your picture taken with them or, if you'd like to get up close and personal with them in the water, you can book a swimming with the dolphins experience. There is also a restaurant serving up fast food on site, as well as a gift shop to buy souvenirs to take home.

Dolphin Bay, at Atlantis The Palm, also offers a range of dolphin experiences, from simple 'meet and greets' through to swimming and scuba diving with the dolphins in the huge purpose-built lagoon.

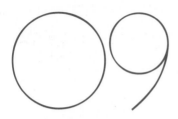

SEGA Republic

Location The Dubai Mall and Dubai Marina Mall **Web** segarepublic.com
Tel 04 448 8488 **Times** 10:00-23:00 (Sunday to Wednesday),
10:00-01:00 (Thursday to Saturday)
Price Guide Dhs.150 **Map** 9 p.216

For an adrenaline-soaring variety of games, rides and simulators that can be enjoyed all year round, you really need look no further than SEGA Republic. In total, there are 150 games that range from virtual ping pong and Guitar Hero to all the latest arcade shoot-em-ups; you can even indulge in a karaoke singalong. And then there are the nine main attractions. Spingear is a full-on white-knuckle rollercoaster, Halfpipe Canyon mixes snowboard skills with a pirate ship, Storm-G is a 360° high-speed bobsleigh simulator, while Initial D4 invites you to get behind the wheel of actual Nissan, Toyota and Subaru touring cars which move, turn and shudder like the real thing as you take on friends and family members over a number of courses. Finally, the Wild Jungle and Wild Wing simulators will have your heart in your mouth from start to finish.

Unlike some other shopping mall amusement centres, SEGA Republic genuinely does appeal to children (and adults) of all ages which makes the Dhs.150 Power Pass (all-day access) pretty good value.

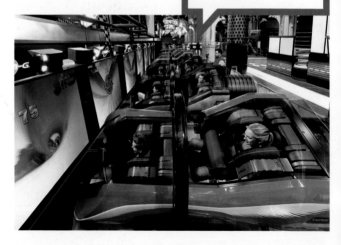

Aquaventure

Location Atlantis The Palm **Web** atlantisthepalm.com
Tel 04 426 0000 **Times** 10.00-sunset (daily)
Price Guide Dhs.165-Dhs.210 **Map** 10 Overview Map

One of the absolute must-do family days out, Aquaventure combines watery fun with plenty of thrills. The Leap of Faith gets the heart beating as you drop 27 metres almost vertically down the side of the Ziggurat pyramid, which is where you'll also find The Plunge and Shark Attack – a slide that shoots you through a tunnel surrounded by shark-infested waters. The Rapids take you on a tumultuous 2.3km journey, complete with waterfalls and wave surges while, for the little ones, there is the Splashers water playground. The 700m long private beach is where mum and dad might like to stretch out and relax while the kids run from slide to slide.

You'll also find Dolphin Bay and The Lost Chambers aquarium within Atlantis, which will both also wow all members of the family. There are tens of restaurants, cafes and snack stands around too.

Discover An Amazing World Where Special Moments Become Lifetime Memories

Come Play For The Day In Atlantis The Palm, Dub

Aquaventure Waterpark:

- The largest waterpark in Dubai
- Over 2 kms of white water rides, slides and rapids
- Access to 700m of private beach

Dolphin Bay:

- The largest man made dolphin habitat in the world
- Dolphin interactions for all ages and swimming abilities
- Includes access to Aquaventure Waterpark and our private beach

For more information or to book your perfect day out, call +971 4 426 0000 or visit atlantisthepalm.com

*Terms and Conditions apply. Interconnecting rooms subject to availability.

he Lost Chambers Aquarium:

- Home to more than 65,000 marine animals
- Explore 10 mysterious, underwater chambers
- Twice daily fish feeding and Aquatheatre shows
- Tours with our Marine Educators

ATLANTIS
THE PALM, DUBAI
atlantisthepalm.com

Showstopper Restaurants

The Observatory

Showstopper
Restaurants
Introduction

Dubai's gastronomic landscape is expansive with celebrity chef and bargain ethnic eateries competing for your hard-earned cash.

Variety is the spice of life where Dubai's restaurant scene is concerned, with all the nationalities that now call this city home all bringing their own particular specialities and flavours to bear on local gastronomy. You will truly find everything from Mexican-inspired molecular gastronomy to back-street Pakistani curry houses, and they're both equally delicious. Many of Dubai's most popular restaurants are located within hotels and leisure clubs, and their popularity is partly down to the fact that these are virtually the only outlets where you can drink alcohol with your meal. Almost all other restaurants are unlicensed. If you're the type who requires a glass of vino to make a meal complete, it's best to phone ahead to check whether the establishment serves alcohol. There's quite a hefty mark-up on drinks, with a decent bottle of wine often costing as much as your meal.

But the city has some superb independent restaurants and cafes that shouldn't be ignored just because they don't serve booze. Some are ethnic eateries in some of Dubai's oldest areas, while others are fresh food cafes and juice bars located in the big malls – all are definitely worth checking out.

However, as much as there are cheap eats and reasonable offers, Dubai is best known for its over-the-top lavishness and this applies to its restaurants as much as everything

else. Big name celebrity chefs rub shoulders with Michelin-starred culinary giants in Dubai, with the likes of Gary Rhodes, Nobu Matsuhisa, Pierre Gagnaire, Richard Sandoval, Sanjeev Kapoor, Marco Pierre White and Giorgio Locatelli all present. These names alone speak volumes about the sheer variety of high-end food on offer in the city. Yet there are the other big names that are just as impressive: restaurants bearing the Armani name, Cavalli Club and the local branches of London's famous Almaz by Momo, The Ivy and Hakkasan – all noted UK celebrity hangouts that add even more glam to Dubai's already glittering offering.

Ramadan Dining

During Ramadan, opening and closing times of restaurants change considerably. Because eating and drinking in public is forbidden during daylight hours, many places only open after sunset then keep going well into the early hours. The breaking of the fast (iftar) is popular with both fasting Muslims and non-fasting expats keen to try the traditional local delicacies, while the practice of suhoor (think of it as the midnight feast that sustains Muslims through the following day's fast) has also become a more communal event that people of all religious backgrounds take part in during Ramadan.

The Observatory

Location Marriott Harbour Hotel & Suites
Web observatory.dubaimarriottharbourhotel.com **Tel** 04 319 4795
Times 17:00-23:00 (daily – bar open till 01:00) **Map** 1 p.219

Given just how many of Dubai's restaurants can boast sensational views, a venue has to be something really special to make it into our Top 10. Fortunately, as the name suggests, The Observatory has arguably the very best view in town. Taking up the entire 52nd floor of the Marriott Harbour Hotel, the main restaurant area looks over Dubai Marina and Media City. It's a view that you'd think you'd have to go a long way to improve upon; in fact, you only need wander as far the bar area (where you can also enjoy lighter nibbles). From here, you can enjoy a bird's eye view over JBR, Dubai International Marine Club and, most impressively of all, The Palm Jumeirah. And you're high up enough to be able to make out the

shape and sheer scope of The Palm in all its illuminated glory. The food is also excellent, mainly based on high-end bistro dishes, such as mussels, carpaccio and baked camembert starters, with main courses of BBQ ribs, surf n turf, red snapper and duck breast. The steaks are superb.

The Observatory is well known for its popular happy hour which offers cocktails at great prices. The happy hour starts at 17:00 and runs until 22:00 Saturday to Tuesday, and until 20:00 Wednesday to Friday.

Teatro

Location Towers Rotana **Web** rotana.com
Tel 04 312 2202 **Times** 18:00-11:30 (daily)
Map 2 p.217

As befits a restaurant that was the brainchild of renowned interior designer Tony Chi, Teatro is, well, theatrical. That said, it's far from showy. The decor is more about an understated sense of drama, with dark colours and vivid reds providing the background, while nods to the name add a little humour to proceedings. Not that Teatro doesn't take its business seriously – both food and drink are of the highest standards here. The restaurant offers a fusion of tastes, with dishes from Japan, China, India and Europe and, whether you go for pizza, noodles, sushi or a curry, the food is guaranteed to please. An open kitchen means you can see the chefs at work

as they prepare your food. There's a wonderful wine collection here – with excellent recommendations always close to hand while, if it's a special occasion, the glass-bound private chef's table is the ideal venue and will make your party the envy of the whole restaurant. The real showstopping element here, however, is the view that the large windows provide of the glimmering Sheikh Zayed Road far below... although the famous sizzling chocolate brownie dessert really does give the view a run for its money when it comes to naming the main attraction here. It may be one of the oldest of Dubai's uber-restaurants, but Teatro still lives up to its billing.

03

Pierchic

Location Al Qasr **Web** jumeirah.com
Tel 04 366 6730 **Times** 13:00-23.30 (daily)
Map 3 p.213

When it comes to compiling a list of restaurants capable of taking the breath away, there are a number of aspects to consider: food, decor, service, location... Some restaurants are included based on a subtle mix of imperceptibles that might go unnoticed by the untrained eye, and then there's Pierchic. Situated at the end of its own beautiful, private wooden pier that juts out 100m or so into the Arabian Gulf, Pierchic sits in a stunningly-designed Arabian-inspired building that is stylish simplicity on the outside and castaway paradise on the outside – where a vast terrace wraps itself around the restaurant. For all that is written about Pierchic, the decor is rarely mentioned and that's for two reasons. Firstly, and most obviously, the views. Looking out to sea in one direction, along the coast to Dubai Marina in another, back to the beautiful Madinat Jumeirah complex and, finally, offering the best, unobstructed views of the Burj Al Arab, few restaurants in the world can claim to be set in a more interesting or varied backdrop. The setting makes Pierchic the ideal setting for couples looking for a romantic evening. Secondly, there's the food. As you'd expect from its location, seafood takes priority here and while it's a long way from your average fish restaurant, the dishes are kept simple but with modern twists. Dishes like tuna carpaccio, freshly-shuckled oysters and pan-fried seabass rely on using the best seasonal ingredients cooked to perfection than any pretentious twists. Desserts are just as good, and the wine menu reads like a sommelier's wish list.

04

Jamie's Italian

Location Festival Centre **Web** jamiesitaliangcc.com
Tel 04 232 9969 **Times** 12:00-23:00 (Saturday to Wednesday),
12:00-00:00 (Thursday to Friday)
Map **4** p.223

Unlike the celeb chefs who arrived in Dubai before him, Jamie Oliver has opted not to chase after the big bucks, but has instead gone for the mid-range and family markets with Jamie's Italian. The restaurant has a mix of industrial and chic, homely decor with vast dangling chandeliers contrasting with sturdy wooden tables. There's a mezzanine level, a busy main dining room and a cosy terrace on the Marina Walk where, tucked behind a garden trellis, you can enjoy a glass of vino with your tasty pumpkin risotto. The menu is good, old-fashioned hearty Italian fare, featuring some outstanding antipasti and a selection of tasty traditional and innovative pastas which come chunky and fresh – the rigatoni is big enough to lose a meatball inside – while the mains cover the usual suspects, like burgers, steaks and Jamie's signature baked fish parcel. The selection of desserts is as extensive – and mouthwatering – as you'll find anywhere. Granted, this is a franchise, but it really feels as though some serious love and care has gone into this venture and the real casual atmosphere makes it great for families too.

Top 10 Family Venues

Hard Rock Café Map **11** p.223
Festival City – 04 399 2888
Go West Map **12** p.213
Jumeirah Beach Hotel – 04 406 8999
Johnny Rockets
Map **13** p.211, 213, 216, 217, 223
Various locations – johnnyrockets.com
The Boardwalk Map **14** p.218
Dubai Creek Golf Club – 04 295 6000
Irish Village Map **15** p.219
The Aviation Club – 04 282 4750
Al Badia Golf Club Brunch Map **16** p.223
Nr Festival City – 04 601 0102
Spice Island Map **17** p.219
Crowne Plaza Deira – 04 262 5555
More Café Map **18** p. 213, 216, 217, 223
Various locations – morecafe.biz
Shakespeare & Co.
Map **19** p.211, p.216, p.217, p.221
Various locations – shakespeareandco.ae
Mazina Family Brunch Map **20** p.211
The Address Dubai Marina – 04 888 3444

From t-shirts, books and DVDs to mugs, aprons and oven gloves, the Jamie goodies available from the restaurant make great gifts.

05

At.mosphere

Location Burj Khalifa **Web** atmosphereburjkhalifa.com
Tel 04 888 3444 **Times** 12:30-23:30 (daily)
Map 5 p.216

There are showstopping restaurants and then there are record-breaking restaurants and, standing at a height of 442m on level 122 of the Burj Khalifa, At.mosphere is officially the highest restaurant in the world. Reason enough to visit, but the wonder goes beyond the stupendous views over Downtown Dubai and along the coast. The kitchen delivers on the lofty ambition, with opulent menus of premium ingredients and exquisite presentation. The Grill is open for lunch and dinner and is the equal of any of the UAE's top restaurants both in flavour and price tag. This really is the ultimate in high-end dining – and has to be the finest sundowners spot on the planet.

The Lounge is open from midday to 02:00 for drinks and snacks; it is also where you can enjoy a really 'high tea' which is a more affordable option for enjoying the cuisine and the views.

06

Hakkasan

Location Jumeirah Emirates Towers **Web** hakkasan.com
Tel 04 384 8484 **Times** 12:00-01:00 (daily)
Map 6 p.217

What works in London or NYC doesn't always translate to Dubai, but Hakkasan is a textbook example of how it can be done. Using familiar Hakkasan elements like the neon bar and the 'cage' design, there are also new introductions, like the 'sunrise' bar (pictured) and, spectacularly, the terrace – a tranquil Zen garden that is unlike anywhere else in Dubai. The Hakkasan favourites are on the menu: starters like crispy

stewed wagyu beef steal most of the plaudits, although the dim sum defines melt in the mouth and the main courses – Pipa duck, sweet and sour pomegranate chicken, and spicy black pepper rib-eye – are best ordered to share. The menu is huge, as is the wine list. Service is charming, knowledgeable and attentive, while the atmosphere balances fine dining and fun. Expensive, but as good as dining

Al Mahara

Location Burj Al Arab **Web** jumeirah.com
Tel 04 301 7600 **Times** 12:30-00:00 (daily)
Map 7 p.213

It has become an icon of modern Dubai, a symbol that is recognised the world over, and, no matter how many people you ask to describe the Burj Al Arab to you, the word 'understated' will never be uttered. And so it goes with Al Mahara – the Burj's flagship seafood restaurant. For starters, there's the fact that your visit starts with a simulated submarine ride 'under the sea', which delivers you to a beautiful cave-like entrance from where you're whisked to your table. Then there's the restaurant itself, which is curled around a giant floor-to-ceiling aquarium which contains sharks, rays and thousands of other fish, which watch you eat while you stare back in amazement. The fine dining menu is predominantly seafood and, once you tear yourself away from the aquarium and concentrate on the food, you'll find sensationally-prepared, quality dishes, such as Alaskan king crab and Japanese scallops; there's even a whole page of the menu dedicated

solely to the different types of caviar on offer. If the caviar takes a whole page, you can only imagine how exhaustive the wine list is. The experience is both sensational and surreal but, most significantly, both food and service are beyond reproach. From start to finish, the staff treat you as though you are a VIP and the only people in the restaurant – the flip side is that this is all reflected in the bill. But then again, you're paying for the uniqueness of the restaurant as much as what you consume; it truly is a once-in-a-lifetime dining experience.

> Gentlemen are required to wear a collared shirt and a jacket to dine at Al Mahara. Ladies, it can get a little cold in the restaurant but the waiters are on hand with pashminas if you do feel the chill.

08
Zuma

Location Dubai International Financial Centre (DIFC)
Web zumarestaurant.com
Tel 04 425 5660 **Times** 12:30-00:00 (Saturday to Wednesday),
12:30-01:00 (Thursday to Friday)
Map 8 p.217

The whole Japanese fusion thing has been done to death now, and it can be easy to dismiss any restaurant that adheres to that template as just following fashion; but Zuma is where that fashion very first began. The restaurant-meeting place made quite a splash when it was one of the first restaurants to open in the trendy new DIFC area; the shock and awe offensive continued when people got a look inside. The stunning multi-level space is elegantly lit, with clean lines of wood and glass creating a restaurant and bar that has stepped straight out of London. It's a huge area but it needs to be – Zuma's carved a reputation of being one of the coolest spots in Dubai at any time of day. It's buzzy, stylish and perfect for a first date or business lunch while, by night, it's where all the beautiful people come to be seen. There are some excellent lunchtime offers, while the Friday brunch is arguably the tastiest in town. Food arrives from the open kitchen and sushi bar artistically presented in classic Japanese style –it's all about simplicity, flair and sharing.

A little different from the usual buffet and cooking station affairs, Friday brunch at Zuma (Dhs.385 including house beverages) is a la carte – the main courses being delivered to your table.

BiCE Mare

Location Souk Al Bahar **Web** bicemare.com
Tel 04 423 0982 **Times** 12:00-00:30 (daily)
Map 9 p.216

The sister to BiCE – one of Dubai's most well-established fine dining restaurants – this is every bit its equal. The 'mare' part of the name signifies a seafood dominated menu of delicious dishes, both simple and complex, that bring fish lovers back time and time again. Aside from the seafood theme, the food on offer also has something of an Italian twist but is genuine and flavourful Italian rather than pizzas and spag bol. You can choose to dine inside and be entertained by the sultry jazz hands of the resident pianist but that would be to miss the point a little. The terrace of BiCE Mare offers one of the best views of the mesmerising Dubai Fountain show which is every bit as dramatic as the tastes on offer here. Start your meal with a limoncello aperitif as you take in the first fountain show and then build to a rousing crescendo in the form of one of the stunning, and massive, seafood platters.

BiCE Mare has a lovely set menu available for Dhs.295 (without alcohol) or Dhs.395 (with house beverages) which allows you to try a little of everything if the menu proves a little too expansive and you're not sure what to plump for.

Vu's Restaurant

Location Jumeirah Emirates Towers **Web** jumeirah.com
Tel 04 319 8088 **Times** 12:30-00:00 (Sunday to Thursday),
19:30-00:00 (Friday & Saturday)
Map 10 p.217

Emirates Towers may not be the latest big building on the block but the sloping roofs of the twin towers are still an icon of Dubai's skyline. Equally, Vu's is hardly a new addition to the city's culinary scene but that doesn't mean the menu is any less fresh – a creative, confident menu, that displays a pure enthusiasm and passion for Asian culinary techniques makes Vu's a place that you could never tire of visiting. The dishes – all exquisitely presented – are mostly modern

European, but come with clever twists. Signature lobster and roast pigeon dishes, as well as the camel's milk and pistachio risotto with Turkish fig cream are delicious. Portions leave you able to move – just as well as you'll want a few angles on the best city light's view of Dubai. With a clean and classic interior, a low-key backing track and dim lighting, Vu's lets the food and the 50th floor location do the persuading. It comes at a tall price, but it's one that is worth paying.

One of the first Dubai skyscrapers, the attention moved away from Emirates Towers with the opening of bigger, bolder buildings but the venue has been revived of late with the addition of Hakkasan Dubai and The Ivy to its impressive culinary portfolio.

Possibly the best beach bar in the world.

barasti

BARASTI, DUBAI'S ORIGINAL BEACH BAR OPEN WEEK IN WEEK OUT – TIL LATE. JOIN US.

For more information call: Barasti Beach at Le Meridien Mina Seyahi
04-318 1313 or visit www.facebook.com/barastibeach

Best Bars

Best Bars
Introduction

Long gone are the days when Dubai's drinking scene was little more than a sandy backwater of British boozers; welcome to one of the world's most exciting bar scenes.

Perhaps standards are high in Dubai because of the particular demands of the city's utterly unique and multicultural drinking crowd. The city's community is such an eclectic mix of creeds and kinds that there's an incredibly varied range of drink and bar expectations. So, have these expectations been met? Indeed, they have – Dubai has responded to these challenges by 'raising the bars' to create a parade of interesting and atmospheric venues vying to meet every drinker's desire.

From the downright dirty (but fun) dive bars of Bur Dubai to some of the world's most glamorous and renowned party venues, Dubai has it all, with every bar attempting to stand out among the city's five-star fleet. Maybe you're in a boardies and flip flops mood and after a laidback sundowner? Or perhaps you're looking to throw on your swankiest threads and plan to take to the town for a raucous Las Vegas style night that you'll never remember? The city bows to your every request.

Although, due to the taxes levied on alcohol, drinking in Dubai can be fairly costly, the city is also bulging with inventive promotions and theme nights that allow you to get merry without paying over the odds. The fairer sex, in particular, can paint the town red without spending a fil thanks to the whole host of drink-specific ladies nights that take place during the week – usually Monday, Tuesday or Wednesday.

When it comes to bar itineraries, Dubai can offer a more varied night out than many other cities, since punters are able to hop into a taxi and zoom between bar stools at opposite sides of town quickly and cheaply.

The venues listed in this chapter highlight the various types of bars in Dubai, both in terms of style and location. Obviously, personal preference plays a significant part in such a list, so keep in mind that these were chosen to emphasise the different varieties in the city – there's not just one bar with great views, one place for sundowners or one beach bar to hit for laid-back cocktails – these are just some of the best and most popular haunts.

So, whether you're looking for that quirky one-of-a-kind bar, a suave cigar lounge, an alfresco bar in the middle of the ocean or a sticky floored dingy dive club, Dubai has it all. And if it doesn't exist right now, it probably will next week.

Door Policy

Certain bars and nightclubs have a selective entry policy. Sometimes 'membership' is introduced to control the clientele, but it is often only enforced during busy periods or to disallow entry for certain groups. Large groups (especially those consisting of all males) and singles, for example, may be turned away from busier bars and clubs without much of an explanation. Avoid the inconvenience by breaking the group up or by going in a mixed-gender group. Some of the city's most popular hotspots, such as 360° (p.78), can be nearly impossible to enter on certain nights unless you're on the guest list so be sure to call and book in advance.

BarZar

Location Souk Madinat Jumeirah **Web** jumeirah.com
Tel 04 366 6730 **Times** 18.00-03.00 (Sunday-Thursday),
12:00-03:00 (Friday & Saturday)
Map 1 p.213

Souk Madinat Jumeirah is a popular spot for entertainment and nightlife, with many lively bars to head to for an evening tipple or to party away the night at. One of the most popular and casual venues is Bar Zar, a funky two-tiered bar that hits the right balance between laidback cool and noisy night-out revelry. Crowds are drawn here largely by the excellent range of drinks promotions on offer right throughout the week. It's also possible to snack on some deep-fried pub grub if hunger sets in, although BarZar is certainly not a restaurant. Major sports events are shown on TVs around the bar, there's a very popular live band that performs most nights of the week on the stage at the back of the bar, and, when the weather's cool, and there's space, you can head outside and chill out on a bean bag overlooking the beautiful waterways that meander through the Souk. One of the best pre-club spots.

O2

Barasti

Location Le Meridien Mina Seyahi Beach Resort & Marina
Web barastibeach.com **Tel** 04 318 1313
Times 11:00-01:30 (Saturday to Wednesday),
11:00-03:00 (Thursday & Friday)
Map 2 p.211

What's not to love about Barasti? Hearty fare, an extensive drinks list at decent prices, open-air live music, beachside DJ parties, shisha on the huge deck or drinks on the beach beanbags... it's really no wonder that Barasti has become a Dubai institution. Especially when you add its convenient Dubai Marina location. The biggest appeal, however, lies in Barasti's 'anything goes' atmosphere which makes it the go-to location for almost any occasion. Expats flock there in anything from straight-off-the-beach flip-flops and boardies to their Friday finery. Split into two levels, with a huge range of areas, Barasti is a beach restaurant by day and early evening – serving up good seafood, ribs, steak and burgers – but, as the sun sets, both levels fill out and the bar transforms into a night venue to suit all tastes. The friendly crowd, gorgeous view, laid back vibe and variety of music played make this one of the city's most reliable spots for a good night out.

As one of the only beach clubs to offer free entrance to non-hotel guests, Barasti is a great haunt for sunbathing. And, should you start to feel peckish, you can refuel upstairs.

As well as the great views and excellent food, it's the laidback charm that draws the crowds to Barasti.

Dubai may be known for its glitz and glamour but there are plenty of more chilled-out and less spendy options. Barasti certainly falls into that category. Plus, you're guaranteed a good atmosphere any day (or night) of the week.

Aprés

Location Mall Of The Emirates **Web** emiratesleisureretail.com
Tel 04 341 2575 **Times** 11.30-01.00 (Saturday to Wednesday),
11.30-02.00 (Thursday & Friday)
Map 3 p.213

It's hard to imagine that a bar
fashioned after an alpine cabin,
overlooking a faux ski slope, set in
a shopping mall, in the middle of
the desert, would work, but Après
manages it with style. The cosy spot
has a comfortable bar area and
amazing views of Ski Dubai (p.144).
The varied menu offers wholesome
fare including steaks, fondue and
pizzas that are big enough to refuel
any tired shopper or snowboarder,
while a couple of the super-strength
cocktails are more than enough to
warm your cockles. So, should you
fancy partying like you're on the piste
at a European ski resort, head to this
slightly insane but perfectly fun venue
'avant' as well as 'apres' ski.

If you find yourself in Dubai
at Christmas, Apres offers
the best festive atmosphere
in the city. With a giant
Christmas tree, wintry feel
and barrels of mulled-wine,
you'll think you're in the
heart of the Alps.

The Jetty Lounge

Location One&Only Royal Mirage **Web** oneandonlyresorts.com
Tel 04 399 9999 **Times** vary according to season
Map 4 p.212

Great views are a dirham a dozen in Dubai, but there are few that offer panoramas paired with chic beachside lounging to match those of Jetty Lounge. Located along the gorgeous calm shores just off the One&Only Royal Mirage, this gem is the perfect post-work hangout, or a delightful night cap venue. Surrounded by contemporary Arabian architecture, select members of the city's laidback crowd perch on the high tables nearest to the bustling bar inside, or,

if the weather is cool enough and space permits, visitors flock outside. The stylish white seating area offers breathtaking views of The Palm. Order a summery mojito from the Hawaiian shirt-clad waiters, sample a few of the tasty appetisers such as mezze, Spanish ham and cheeses or Asian-inspired platters, listen to the sounds of chilled out beach tunes, and you'll almost immediately feel the vacation vibe flow over you – whether you're on holiday or not.

As the name suggests, Jetty Lounge features a wooden jetty that juts out into the sea. Should you feel like bar hopping, jump aboard a private boat that will take you to the sister hotel, One&Only The Palm, where another bar with sea views awaits.

O5

Skyview Bar

Location Burj Al Arab **Web** jumeirah.com
Tel 04 301 7600 **Times** 12:00-02:00 (daily, except Friday)
Map 5 p.213

A trip to Dubai is simply not complete without having experienced sundowners at the top of Burj Al Arab. The bar itself, perched at the very top of the hotel which sits on its own man-made island, offers gorgeous views of the city, and, provided you come before sunset, it's possible to make out The World Islands in the hazy distance. Like the hotel, the decor was never intended to be understated; the ceiling is lit up with primary coloured ripples and the carpet, a dizzying array of multi-coloured swirls, makes for a dazzling disco effect. While a cocktail here can easily run into triple figures, it's worth it for special occasions or to impress out-of-town visitors. It is a quintessential Dubai experience after all. Just remember you'll have to plan in advance and book early. There's also a minimum spend of Dhs.275 per person just to get in.

It may be an expensive cuppa, but indulging in afternoon tea at Skyview Bar will make for one of your most memorable holiday experiences. It begins with a glass of bubbly and continues with a delectable serving of sandwiches, scones and other fine pastries. Afternoon tea here costs Dhs.425 per person.

360°

Location Jumeirah Beach Hotel
Web jumeirah.com
Tel 04 406 8999
Times 17.00-02.00
(Sunday to Wednesday),
17.00-03.00
(Thursday to Saturday),
16:00–03.00 (Friday)
Map 6 p.213

Located on a private jetty, just off the coast of the Jumeirah Beach Hotel, 360° is the type of bar that keen partygoers cross continents to find. It delivers exactly what the name might suggest: superb 360 degree panoramas of Dubai's burgeoning skyline with, most notably, the Burj Al Arab within grasping distance. Set on a circular rooftop, almost completely surrounded by water on all sides, the decor is all white, with leather sofas and cabanas – ideal for reclining on as you sip on the best sundowner you may ever enjoy. Early evening is what 360° was made for. However, as the night turns into early morning, an entirely different crowd heads to 360° as the popular house DJs spin until the early hours. For a little dose of Arabian culture, opt for a flavoured shisha to accompany your cocktail.

07
Neos

Location The Address Downtown Dubai **Web** theaddress.com
Tel 04 436 8888 **Times** 18.00-02.00 (daily)
Map 7 p.216

As you make your way up 63 floors to the very top of The Address Downtown, you could be forgiven for thinking that you've also stepped back in time as you emerge into this glamorous, art deco themed bar. Drag your eyes away from the stunning view of the Burj Khalifa opposite to take in the extensive menu of well executed cocktails and small bites which includes wagyu beef skewers, oysters and a caviar menu. Top-end ingredients and unusual concoctions mean a heftier price tag than what you may find elsewhere but it's a great Downtown option if you're looking for the perfect Dubai Fountain view. Choose between the cosy, low level velvet seating or sit close to the action on bar stools for a more sophisticated and lively evening. Either way, the service is top notch and the atmosphere chic, so sit back and let the pianist create the perfect mood music for an elegant night out. The dress code here is glamorous, so throw on your finery. Reservations are recommended for that coveted window seat for the best view of The Dubai Fountain.

For a livelier night or an alfresco evening, stop off at the 5th floor and visit Calabar (same number and website as above) in The Address Downtown Dubai. This premium lounge bar attracts Dubai's fashionable elite, and its gorgeous terrace comes alive at sunset.

Siddharta Lounge
By Buddha Bar

Location Grosvenor House **Web** grosvenorhouse-dubai.com
Tel 04 317 6000 **Times** 19:00-00:00 (daily)
Map 8 p.211

Whether you're in search of a stylish venue that serves delicious food and fancy cocktails, or you're looking for a great spot to see and be seen, Siddharta Lounge is hard to beat for wow factor. The restaurant-bar-lounge, which opened in 2011 at Grosvenor House Tower 2, has its own private entrance for outside guests and is a new favourite after-dark playground for Dubai's glamorous and well-heeled crowd. Siddharta Lounge boasts a sleek and contemporary interior, featuring ample lashings of plush white seating, gold accents and glam marble furnishings, coupled with floor-to-ceiling windows that reveal stunning views of Dubai Marina. Decor aside, the food and drinks on offer are where the venue really excels. You'll be spoilt for choice with a menu that features a mouth-watering selection of Asian-Mediterranean specialities, including wagyu beef mini burgers, and crispy prawn spring rolls with tamarind dipping sauce. The chef's selection of desserts is also outstanding; notably the delicious three-chocolate terrine with caramelised banana.

If you fancy an alfresco evening, head outside to the elegant pool terrace to enjoy the picturesque views of Dubai Marina. The seating area is as sleek as it is cosy, with white day beds to lounge on while chatting with friends.

As one of the first luxury hotels
to arrive in Dubai's stylish Marina
neighbourhood, the Grosvenor
House has set the standard for
luxurious, jet-set living in Dubai.

Siddarta Lounge joins an already impressive list of chic bars
inside the hotel which include the perennial favourite Buddha Bar
(pictured) and the new, chic South American venue Toro Toro.

09

QD's

Location Dubai Creek Golf & Yacht Club **Web** dubaigolf.com
Tel 04 295 6000 **Times** 17:00-02:00 (daily)
Map 9 p.218

During summer, when Dubai's residents are either swimming in sweat or stuck inside an air-conditioned cell, a night at QD's seems like a distant dream. But from October through to May, this ultimate sundowner spot is pure, delightful reality. Pull up a padded chair on the banks of the creek, so close to the water's edge that you'll want to dip your feet in, and watch the passing abras as the sun sets over Sheikh Zayed Road from this charming and atmospheric locale. Delicious bar snacks and pizzas accompany an excellent cocktail list and, as the night wears on, the live band keeps the shisha-smoking, uber laid-back crowd entertained. Dubai may be sprawling from its traditional centre, but QD's is at the heart of its simple pleasures.

QD's is the ideal casual evening out where beers and bar snacks trump fancy cocktails and glamorous rags. If you're looking for heartier fare, however, Boardwalk (same contact details) is right next door.

Aquara

Location Dubai Marina Yacht Club **Web** dubaimarinayachtclub.com
Tel 04 362 7900 **Times** 19:00-00:00 (daily), 12:30-15:30 (Friday Brunch)
Map 10 p.211

You'd be forgiven for thinking you were in the midst of a summer's evening in Monaco at this chic yet understated bar in the heart of New Dubai. Overlooking the gorgeous marina, with its million-dirham yachts lined up for all to see, and overshadowed by the imposing residential skyscrapers in the background, it's difficult not to be enthralled by the lavishness of it all. If you can tear your eyes away from the glittering promenade and shimmery waters, you'll find a bar filled with Dubai residents and visitors kicking back and letting loose. And while the drinks here are particularly delectable – there's a happy hour every day from 18:00 to 20:00 – the food shouldn't be missed either. Offering a seafood-inspired menu with an Asian twist, you can choose to sit indoors in a pleasant and cosy atmosphere, or unwind on the unforgettable alfresco terrace. Friday Brunch is a speciality at Aquara, featuring an oyster and seafood bar, sushi counter, carving stations and other tasty delicacies to whet your appetite. It may be one of the older bars in the Dubai Marina area, but it has maintained a good following of loyal clientele who love the picture-postcard views.

"It's one thing to know how to play like an expert and quite another to do it all the time."

Cecilia Le
National SCRABBLE Championship
Winner 2006

Jashanmal
books.com

Shopping
Spots

Shopping

Shopping

Spice Souk

Shopping
Spots
Introduction

With souks, boutiques and mammoth malls at every turn, you won't have any problems spending your hard-earned cash while out and about in Dubai.

Dubai provides many opportunities to indulge in a shopping spree: with countless malls, souks and markets to choose from, the desert city is a true shopaholic's dream where you can buy just about anything.

Dubai is world-famous for its modern mega-malls, such as The Dubai Mall (p.92) and Mall of the Emirates (p.93). These gleaming hubs of trade are filled with a mix of international high street brands and plush designer names. Practicality plays a large part in Dubai's mall culture and during the hotter months, the malls are oases of cool in the sweltering city, somewhere to walk, shop, eat and be entertained away from the soaring heat outside.

But shopping in Dubai is not just about mall-trawling. Indeed, some of the city's best shopping spots are to be found outside the malls – venture a bit further and you can find yourself in an atmospheric souk shopping for spices or gold (p.101). The souks, Arabia's traditional market places provide a slightly more original way to shop; bargaining is very much a part of the experience and instead of branded stores, you'll find small independent shopkeepers and stalls marketing their wares in an atmospheric setting.

In addition to specialist souks, there are a number of places where a broad range of items, including souvenirs and traditional gifts, are sold. Shopping spots such as Karama (p.96), Khan Murjan (p.95) and Satwa (p.98) are examples of places where you can shop to your heart's content in a non-mall setting.

Bargaining is still common practice in the souks and other traditional shopping areas of the UAE; you'll need to give it a go to get the best prices. Before you take the plunge, try to get an idea of prices from a few shops, as there can often be a significant difference. Once you've decided how much you are willing to spend, offer an initial bid that is roughly around half that price. Stay laidback and vaguely disinterested in general. When your initial offer is rejected (and it will be), keep going until you reach an agreement or until you have reached your own limit. If the price isn't right, say so and walk out – the vendor will often follow and suggest a compromise price. As a general rule, the more you buy, the better the discount. When the price is agreed, it is considered bad form to back out of the sale.

Shopping Hours

Dubai is the promised land of shopping and with most stores open seven days a week, you'll find no trouble tracking down your desired goods. And with most shops open from around 09:00 until at least 22:00 every night, and some until midnight at the weekends, there's plenty of time to browse.

01

Souk Madinat Jumeirah

Location Al Sufouh 1 **Web** jumeirah.com
Tel 04 366 8888 **Times** 10:00-22:00 (daily)
Map 1 p.213

Souk Madinat Jumeirah is a recreation of a traditional souk, complete with narrow alleyways, authentic architecture and motorised abras. The blend of outlets is unlike anywhere else in Dubai, with boutique shops, galleries, cafes, restaurants and bars. This is a great spot to stock up on souvenirs and art with a regional flair. In the outside areas and all along the winding corridors, you'll find stalls selling all manner of souvenir staples – some tasteful and some tacky. For something classy, the souk is also home to a concentration of art boutiques, including Gallery One (04 368 6055), which sells photos with a local flavour, and Spirit of Art Gallery (04 368 6207). For holiday clobber, eye-catching but expensive swimming gear can be found at Vilebrequin (04 368 6531), Rodeo Drive (04 368 6568) and Tommy Bahama (04 368 6031). You can also sample colourful embroidered tunics that make a great beach cover-up. All that shopping may make you hungry, and luckily the souk is home to dozens of waterfront cafes, bars and restaurants to choose from. Try the Agency (04 368 6171) for drinks or tuck into some hearty European fare at the Belgian Beer Café (belgianbeercafe.com).

O2
The Dubai Mall

Location Downtown Dubai
Web thedubaimall.com
Tel 800 38224 6255
Times 10:00-22:00 (Sunday to Wednesday),
10:00-00:00 (Thursday to Saturday)
Map 2 p.216

The Dubai Mall is one of the world's largest shopping centres; home to some 1,200 stores, countless eateries and enough leisure draws to satisfy even the most demanding of shoppers, this is a true lifestyle destination. The shopping highlights are manifold, but unique to Dubai Mall are the regional flagship stores for New York department store Bloomingdale's, French department store Galeries LaFayette (04 339 9933), the world-renowned toy shop Hamleys (04 339 8889) and UK upmarket food retailer Waitrose (04 434 0700). You'll find all of the haute couture designer brands along Fashion Avenue and there is a sprawling gold souk with over 220 gold and jewellery outlets. Shopping aside, the huge complex houses attractions such as an Olympic size ice skating rink (p.41), a catwalk for fashion shows, an enormous aquarium (p.40), a 22 screen cinema, an indoor theme park called SEGA Republic (p.44), a luxury hotel, and the children's edutainment centre KidZania (p.35). Given its gigantic dimensions, it could be easy to get lost inside the mall. However, touch-screen maps and knowledgeable staff make it easy to find your way around the shops and other draws, while most stores are gathered by type. For a complete contrast, cross the wooden bridge over the Burj Khalifa Lake and you'll find yourself in the soothing Souk Al Bahar (p.99). The tranquillity of its dimly lit passageways offers a more relaxing stop after the onslaught of the big, bright mall.

10 Other Malls Not To Miss

Mall of the Emirates Map **11** p.213
malloftheemirates.com
Festival Centre Map **12** p.223
festivalcentre.com
Ibn Battuta Mall Map **13** p.210
ibnbattutamall.com
Wafi Map **14** p.218
wafi.com
Dubai Marina Mall Map **15** p.211
dubaimarinamall.com
Lamcy Plaza Map **16** 218
lamcyplaza.com
BurJuman Map **17** p.218
burjuman.com
Deira City Centre Map **18** p.219
deiracitycentre.com
Mercato Map **19** p.217
mercatoshoppingmall.com
Mirdif City Centre Map **20** p.223
mirdifcitycentre.com

JBR Walk

Location Dubai Marina
Times 10:00-22:00 (Sunday to Thursday), 10:00-00:00 (Friday & Saturday)
Map 3 p.211

A solution to the age-old gripe that there aren't enough places to walk in Dubai: The Walk, Jumeirah Beach Residence (JBR) is a move away from glitzy mall interiors and towards street-side shops and cafes. The fully pedestrianised area stretches 1.7 kilometres along the beachfront and strolling from one end to the other will take you past a host of retail options. The shops range from clothing to interior decoration and watersports specialist gear. Outlets are located either on the ground level or on the plaza level of six clusters of towers called Murjan, Sadaf, Bahar, Rimal, Amwaj and Shams. Fashion forward shoppers will be pleased with stores like Boutique 1 (boutique1.com) and Saks Fifth Avenue (saksfifthavenue. com). There is also a branch of ACT Marine (04 424 3191), which sells a good range of equipment for watersports, should you wish to test the turquoise waters crashing onto the sand just steps away on JBR's popular open beach. Most shops open at 10:00 and

close at 22:00. For a well-deserved pit-stop in between shopping, you'll get to choose from the countless cafes and restaurants scattered all along the bustling promenade. During the cooler months of the year, the shopping options are more varied still thanks to Covent Garden Market. Every week (Wednesday to Saturday), the area in front of Rimal transforms into a vibrant street market when countless stalls and stands turn up to sell their wares. This is a great place to pick up some local art, unique clothing or hand-made jewellery, with plenty of souvenirs to boot.

Khan Murjan

Location Wafi 2 **Web** wafi.com
Tel 04 324 4555 **Times** 10:00-22:00 (Saturday to Wednesday),
10:00-00:00 (Friday & Thursday)
Map 4 p.218

For something a little different, head to Wafi's underground souk. Located directly underneath one of Dubai's most luxurious malls, Khan Murjan feels a world away from the gleaming designer stores upstairs – take the escalators found at Wafi mall's Atrium or Colonnade to find this subterranean shopping spot which is easily among the city's most atmospheric and memorable shopping spots. Khan Murjan's magnificent stained glass ceiling (which stretches 64m) and long, curved arches help make this a truly unique place to engage in a bit of retail therapy. The goods you can expect to bag here do not fall in the standard shopping mall category either: the souk features over 150 stalls selling everything from jewellery to antiques and Arabic perfume, so

you're guaranteed to walk away with something that ranks high in terms of colour and local flair. This is the place to head to if you want to find souvenirs or gifts. Think ornamental Arabic slippers, gorgeous drop earrings or exotic, fragrant frankincense. Khan Murjan is a particularly good bet if you wish to spice your home with traditional arts and crafts, or to bring something truly special back home. In addition to the wide selection that's yours to sample at the various stalls, there are occasionally workshops where skilled artisans can create various bits of arts and crafts on site to your own personal spec. In the centre of the souk, you'll find an open air marble courtyard which houses the highly recommended Khan Murjan Arabic restaurant (04 327 9795).

Karama

Location Al Karama
Map 5 p.218

This is one of the best places in town to find a bargain. The Karama Complex (often referred to as Karama Market), a long street which runs through the middle of the district, is lined by shops on both sides and, whether it's bargain clothing, sports goods, gifts or souvenirs you're after, you'll find it here. There's a huge range of T-shirts, shoes, shorts and sunglasses at very reasonable prices and two of the most popular shops for these are Blue Marine and Green Eye. Just around the corner, the imaginatively named Asda offers handbags and accessories over two floors; it's pretty claustrophobic but the range is excellent and the prices won't break the bank. For souvenirs, Gifts Tent (04 335 4416) is one of the larger outlets. The selection includes pashminas in every shade imaginable. Karama is also the centre of the local counterfeit trade.

06

Global Village

Location Dubailand **Web** globalvillage.ae
Tel 04 362 4114 **Times** 16:00-00:00 (Saturday to Wednesday),
16:00-01:00 (Thursday & Friday)
Price Guide Dhs.5 **Map** 6 p.221

Located on the Emirates Road near Arabian Ranches, Global Village is a huge collection of stalls, eateries and entertainment from all over the world. It runs during the winter months and is a good spot to pick up everything from Chinese lanterns to honey from Yemen. Organised by country, you can spend hours exploring the wares before enjoying a unique range of dishes in the international foodcourt. Just don't overdo dinner before get-

ting on the fairground rides, which include a big wheel and a couple of rollercoasters, as well as some tamer options. Rides, however, are not included in the entry price.

> From November to March, Global Village is among the city's most colourful places for a spot of alfresco shopping.

Satwa

Location Al Satwa
Times 10:00-22:00 (Saturday to Thursday), 10:00-00:00 (Friday & Saturday)
Map 7 p.217

Satwa is one of Dubai's original retail areas, and it has something of a village feel about it, with shoppers able to stock up on just about any everyday essential imaginable, as well as some rarer items. The small stores that line the streets of Satwa retail everything from household appliances to furniture. That said, Satwa is arguably best known for its fabric shops and tailors. Deepa's (04 349 9733), Deepak's (04 344 8836) and Dream Girl Tailors (04 337 7287) are popular and will take on all tailoring jobs from taking up trousers to making superb ball gowns. Al Diyafah Road (now officially called 2nd December Street

but still referred to by its old name by everybody in town) is a great place for a lively evening stroll. There's an eclectic mix of shops and food outlets – expect to find just about anything from formal wear to pots and pans here – and the ambiance makes it well worth the trip.

Shopping aside, the lively streets around Satwa have some good fastfood options. Al Mallah is a popular Lebanese restaurant that enjoys a steady following thanks to its authentic local food, while Ravi's – which serves up curries so good and so cheap that they've become part of Dubai folklore – is also in this area.

Satwa is particularly good for well-priced electronics, such as mobile phones, cameras and even watches. Plant Street, as the name suggests, is a must-stop for horticulturalists, while there are also some great value spas to be found in this area.

Souk Al Bahar

Location Downtown Dubai **Web** soukalbahar.ae
Tel 04 362 7011 **Times** 10:00-22:00 (Saturday to Thursday),
14:00-22:00 (Friday) **Map** 8 p.216

Located just a stone's throw from the modern retail extravaganza of The Dubai Mall (p.92), Souk Al Bahar's atmospheric passageways offer a more tranquil – but certainly no less appealing – shopping experience. Built to resemble a traditional souk, the atmospheric lifestyle destination is home to several shops selling Arabian wares that make excellent souvenirs or gifts. Among the local products you can pick up here are carpets, ornaments, paintings, jewellery, clothes and perfumes, as well as some tackier keepsakes (sheikh and sheikha salt and pepper shakers, for example). For something for the house, look no further than Marina Exotic Home Interiors (marinagulf. com). This upmarket store stocks striking furniture, but also smaller decoration items from beautiful pillows to colourful lanterns that will transform your home in a flash. This souk hardly ever feels too busy, so it is a perfect hideaway if the hectic pace of the surrounding Downtown area has left you weary. Sample the small boutiques, make a stop at one of the many cafes or bars, or simply turn up to admire the fabulous views of Burj Khalifa. There's also a great selection of eateries. Try The Rivington Grill (rivingtongrill.ae) for British dining or sip a coffee at New York's gourmet cafe Dean & DeLuca (04 420 0336).

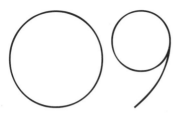

09

Dubai Outlet Mall

Location Dubailand **Web** dubaioutletmall.com
Tel 04 423 4666 **Times** 10:00-22:00 (Saturday to Wednesday),
10:00-00:00 (Thursday & Friday)
Map 9 Overview Map

In a city where the emphasis in on excess, it's refreshing (for the wallet too) to find a mall dedicated to saving money. Dubai's first 'outlet' concept may be a way out of town (20 minutes down the Al Ain road) but it's worth the drive. Big discounts on major retailers and labels are available; think T-shirts for under Dhs.30 and Karama-esque prices for Marc Jacobs handbags. High street shops including Massimo Dutti and Dune sit alongside designer names such as Tommy Hilfiger and DKNY, with city style and sports casual equally catered for. Clothing aside, you can find jewellery from Damas, cosmetics from Paris Gallery and a range of electronics and homeware in various outlets.

Sporty shoppers are particularly well catered for at Dubai Outlet Mall, with Nike, Adidas, Adidas Originals, Reebok, Sketchers, Go Sports, Sports Direct, BH Bikes, Columbia and more.

Gold & Spice Souks

Location Al Ras
Times 10:00-22:00 (Saturday to Thursday),
10:00-00:00 (Friday & Saturday) **Map** 10 p.219

There are a number of souks and markets in Dubai, but few are as authentic and atmospheric as those found in the city's traditional trading areas along the Deira Creek. The Gold and Spice Souks are among the best known and for a very good reason – these shopping hotspots offer an abundance of sights, sounds and smells that are guaranteed to linger in your memory long after the experience. The meandering lanes of the Gold Souk are lined with shops selling elaborate jewellery, pearls and deep-hued gem stones. Gold is sold by weight according to the daily international price and so will be much the same as in the shops in malls – the price of the workmanship is where you will have more bargaining power. Most of the outlets operate split shifts, so try not to visit between 13:00 and 16:00 as some may be closed. Customised pieces can be created according to your requests if you have a few days to spare and the quality of the workmanship is usually very good. Lingering smells of exotic spices lead you in the direction of the Spice Souk. This is a great place to pick up rare treats such as fresh vanilla pods, high-quality saffron or fiery chilli at surprisingly low prices. Bargaining is very much the name of the game in the souks. Arrive with plenty of patience and your most charming smile, and remember that cash always gives you most leverage.

Welcome to a racecourse where everyone wins.

THE MEYDAN
A DESTINATION HOTEL

The Meydan Hotel combines the passion for equestrian sports with world-class luxury and traditional Arabic hospitality. Home to the richest horse race in the world, the hotel has 284 contemporary suites each offering grandstand views. Great restaurants, a new Troon managed golf course, a tennis academy, and an infinity pool offering unparalleled views of the Dubai skyline; make The Meydan a destination hotel unlike any other.

MEYDAN
HOTELS

For more information
call +971 4 381 3231 or
email info@meydanhotels.com

Destination
Hotels

Madinat Jumeirah & Burj Al Arab

Destination Hotels
Introduction

If one aspect of Dubai has come to define both the city and the emirate, it is the array of jaw-dropping hotels that welcome millions of guests each year.

Dubai's hotels don't only provide accommodation and host corporate functions, but they are the hubs around which the local social scene revolves. Hotels here are places where locals pop for a drink; where you'll find the best restaurants for dining out; where you can relax by the beach or engage in a wide range of outdoor and indoor sports. There are literally dozens of the world's leading hotel brands to be found here and, given the important role that hotels play in the lives of both visitors and residents, many of these top hospitality brands are housed in some of the city's most iconic buildings.

In a destination built on superlatives every bit as much as oil, Dubai's hotels certainly play their part. Among the famous names, you'll find some of the world's tallest hotels, and easily many of its most opulent: some are world firsts from legendary fashion brands; some are sprawling resorts connected by kilometres of canals; yet others sit on their own private islands or flank one of the modern wonders of the world, The Palm Jumeirah. Last but not least, a number have been the scene-stealing stars of some big-name movies.

Whether you're staying in one of these architectural wonders or not, you're sure to spend plenty of time in and around a destination hotel as they are where you'll find a number of Dubai's main attractions, from Aquaventure waterpark (p.45) at Atlantis, The Palm to the creekside

bars (p.84) of the beautiful Park Hyatt (p.144). Plus, like the vast majority of Dubai's hotels, all of these destination hotels take part in the famous Friday Brunch (p.184) which is a great way to check out one of these places if you've not yet had the chance to visit.

A few of the hotels featured in this Top 10 sit right on the Arabian Gulf and, if you're not staying at the hotel, you can still get a day pass that will allow you to enjoy the private beach, pool, sun loungers and other facilities. The desert hotels can also be enjoyed as a visitor, with many offering luxury takes on Bedouin experiences, including henna, shisha and camel rides along with a traditionally-themed brunch of dinner.

However you choose to enjoy them, try to see as many of these dazzling destination hotels as you can during your visit as they truly are some of Dubai's greatest attractions. The Dubai Department of Tourism & Commerce Marketing operates a centralised internet reservation system for Dubai's hotels at definitelydubai.com.

Summer Surprise
If you live locally, keep your eye out for the special offers that pop up during the hot summer months. GCC residents can often find discounts of up to 50% or room rates that include extra meals, spa treatments or activities – the perfect opportunity to take a bargain break.

The Meydan Hotel

Location Meydan
Web themeydan.com
Tel 04 381 3333
Map 1 Overview Map

A beautiful trackside hotel that combines cutting-edge design with equine touches, The Meydan is the ultimate destination hotel for horse racing lovers. Can there possibly be a cooler place in the world to watch the action than from the rooftop infinity pool of this decadent delight? Almost all of the 285 rooms look out on to the racecourse too. Outside of race season, there's an excellent spa and a couple of exceptional restaurants in the shape of Prime and Shiba. There are also some cracking activities to try, with a nine-hole golf course, tennis academy, as well as the hunting and shooting simulator.

The Meydan Hotel forms one end of the incredible Meydan Grandstand, which can accommodate 60,000 spectators for horse races and is often described as the world's biggest 'landscraper' at 1.6km in length. If you're not watching the Dubai World Cup from the hotel itself, you want to be in the the Sky Bubble – perched on top of the grandstand, it offers 360° views of Dubai.

02

Atlantis, The Palm

Location Palm Jumeirah **Web** atlantisthepalm.com
Tel 04 426 0000
Map 2 Overview Map

With a staggering 1,539 rooms and suites, all with views of the sea or The Palm Jumeirah, Atlantis is certainly one of Dubai's grandest and most recognisable hotels after it was catapulted into the world's consciousness when it opened with a $15 million firework display when it opened in 2008. Sitting at the end of the giant manmade Palm Jumeirah, you can drive or take a taxi to Atlantis, although it's also served by its own monorail. Atlantis is home to a huge number of restaurants, with Ossian, a Seafire Steakhouse, Nobu and Ronda Locatelli, anchored by the Michelin-starred chef Giorgio Locatelli, arguably the highlights. The Friday

Brunch at Saffron is one of Dubai's biggest, tastiest but also wildest. The beach club, Nasimi Beach, is a popular chill-out haunt in the winter evenings and also hosts the giant Sandance series of mini music festivals during the cooler months. Atlantis, The Palm is where you'll find a number of top family attractions such as the Lost Chambers aquarium, which features 20 marine exhibits and 56,000 fish and marine creatures, and Dolphin Bay, where both kids and adults can meet and interact with the dolphins. By far the biggest draw is Aquaventure (p.45), the biggest water park in the Middle East with fun pools, adrenaline slides and long rapids.

Al Maha Desert Resort & Spa

Location Dubailand **Web** al-maha.com
Tel 04 832 9900
Map 3 p.209

Set within the 225 square kilometre Dubai Desert Conservation Reserve and boasting some breathtaking views of picturesque dunes and rare Arabian wildlife, a few years ago this luxury getaway was named as one of the best examples of ecotourism by no less than *National Geographic*. Al Maha is designed to resemble a typical and traditional Bedouin camp, but conditions here are anything but basic. Each suite is beautifully crafted and has its own private pool and butler service. There's a signature restaurant, although deck and dune dining under the stars can also be arranged, while the activities that can be enjoyed include horse riding, camel trekking, nature walks and falconry. There is also a superb spa.

The conservation reserve is a protected area where you'll find many species of Arabian mammals and birds, such as free-roaming herds of endangered oryx.

04

Armani Hotel Dubai

When the legendary Italian brand
Armani chose Dubai as the location for
its first ever hotel, expectations were
set extremely high – almost literally.
Not only has Giorgio Armani himself
designed or chosen every last feature
of the hotel, but Armani Dubai is
located in the lower floors of the Burj
Khalifa – the world's tallest building.
Fortunately, the high profile hotel
does not disappoint. This luxurious,
and, let's face it, expensive hotel is
remarkably without pretension, but
its designer credentials are there for
all to see, right down to the nuts,
bolts and door handles. As well as
elegant suites kitted out with Armani/
Casa goods, the hotel is home to a
clutch of excellent dining venues,
many of which look out over The
Dubai Fountain; there is also the
Armani/Prive lounge bar. Armani/
Spa is a stunning space offering a
wide range of treatments that make
use of Armani's own products; the
Italian brand's traditional 'less is more'
approach mean this is a spa that may
appeal more to the men too.

The rooms and suites in
Armani Dubai contain iPods
featuring a playlist that has
been chosen by Giorgio
Armani himself. The designer
also selected the books that
appear in certain suites.

Downtown Dubai is one of the city's newest areas, encompassing the Burj Khalifa, The Dubai Mall, Souk Al Bahar and a handful of hotels, most of which have spectacular views over The Dubai Fountain.

The record-breaking fountain is 275 metres long and shoots water 150 metres (50 storeys) into the air. There are a number of different 'performances' backed by music ranging from traditional Arabic to classical and show tunes.

05

Park Hyatt Dubai

Location Port Saeed
Web dubai.park.hyatt.com
Tel 04 602 1234
Map 5 p.218

Enjoying a unique and prime waterfront location, within the grounds of Dubai Creek Golf & Yacht Club, the Park Hyatt is a Mediterranean-style resort, with natural colours and stylish decor. Although certainly a high-end offering – as the boats in the neighbouring marina and immaculate golf course suggest – the low-rise style gives it a more laid-back ambience than many of Dubai's other top hotels. The hotel has 225 rooms and suites in total, all with beautiful Dubai Creek views, as well as some great dining outlets and a luxurious spa, which features a luxury couple's massage option. The excellent restaurants inside the hotel include The Thai Kitchen and Traiteur, both of which have extremely popular brunches (p.184).

In the same grounds also lie Boardwalk and QDs (p.84) which share amazing locations, perched over the waters of the creek and are great venues for enjoying food, drink or shisha (p.182) while soaking up city views.

06

Bab Al Shams Desert Resort & Spa

Location Bawadi **Web** meydanhotels.com
Tel 04 809 6100
Map 6 p.209

Bab Al Shams (which means 'The Gateway to the Sun') is a beautiful desert resort built in the style of a traditional Arabic fort. Each of its 115 rooms is decorated with subtle yet stunning Arabian touches, and the surrounding pristine desert dunes form the backdrop. The authentic, open-air, Arabic restaurant is highly recommended, although Le Dune pizzeria is also popular. There is a kids' club, a large swimming pool (complete with swim-up bar), lawn games and the luxurious Satori Spa, while everything from morning yoga to desert safaris can be organised.

Burj Al Arab

Location Umm Suqeim 3 **Web** jumeirah.com
Tel 04 301 7777
Map 7 p.213

What can be said that's not already been said about the hotel that redefined the word 'luxury' and has become a symbol for Dubai's rise to prominence? Standing on its own man-made island, this dramatic Dubai icon's unique architecture is now recognised around the world. Every suite in the hotel spans two floors and is serviced by a team of butlers. To get into the hotel as a non-guest, you will need a restaurant reservation – afternoon tea in Sahn Eddar or Skyview Bar are popular options for those wanting to take a look around. The Assawan Spa & Health Club also covers a couple of floors, offering opulent treatments as well as gyms, pools and a squash court, and there is also a completely private stretch of beach reserved for guests. The hotel is linked by a bridge to the Madinat Jumeirah resort (p.119) and Wild Wadi waterpark (p.34).

XVA Art Hotel

Location Al Souk Al Kabeer **Web** xvahotel.com
Tel 04 353 5383
Map 8 p.218

Located in the centre of Bastakiya, one of the city's oldest areas, this is one of Dubai's most interesting, not to mention hippest, hotels. The building itself was originally a traditional windtower house, but it has since been fully restored and, in addition to the hotel, XVA contains an internationally-acclaimed art gallery, a popular vegetarian cafe, a number of stores and even an in-house tailor. The hotel is one of very few in Dubai that can genuinely lay claim to the 'boutique' label, with just eight bedrooms that surround three open courtyards. Each of the bedrooms at XVA Hotel has been designed by a local artist or interior designer, with modern finishes meeting traditional styles and influences throughout.

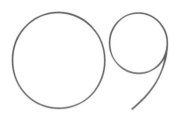

09
Jumeirah Zabeel Saray

Location Palm Jumeirah **Web** jumeirahzabeelsaray.com
Tel 04 453 0000
Map 9 p.211

Zabeel Saray is something of a structural wonder, combining Arabian and Turkish influences to create a hotel that screams luxury. Located on the crescent of The Palm Jumeirah, the hotel has its own private stretch of beach that looks back over the Palm, with several of its food and drink outlets boasting terraced areas that enjoy the same view. Of the restaurants, Amala and Voi are perhaps the highlights, although it's also well worth popping in for afternoon tea at Sultan's Lounge or a nighttime cocktail in the too-cool Voda Bar. The main attraction at Zabeel Saray, however, is the Talise Ottoman Spa around which the rest of the hotel is built.

With 50 treatment rooms, mineral pools, majlis areas, saunas, ice chambers, couples' suites, gyms and stunning hammams, the spa here lays claim to being the biggest in the Middle East and one of the largest in the world.

10

Madinat Jumeirah

Location Al Sufouh 1 **Web** jumeirah.com
Tel 04 366 8888
Map 10 p.213

Madinat Jumeirah is more of a sprawling resort than a traditional hotel. Located right next to Burj al Arab and Wild Wadi (it's all part of the same Jumeirah Group), the Madinat actually encompasses two large hotels, Al Qasr and Mina A'Salam – with no fewer than 940 luxurious rooms and suites between them – as well as the exclusive Dar Al Masyaf summer houses, which have their own private swimming pools, although the hotels do also share a vast stretch of private beach and one of the region's biggest swimming pools. There is a large Talise Spa and a state-of-the-art health club in the resort, and the whole area

is linked by an incredible system of man-made waterways that are navigated by the wooden abra boats that whisk guests around the resort. For those not staying at either hotel – or tackling the legendary Al Qasr brunch (p.184) – the biggest draw is Souk Madinat Jumeirah. Based on a traditional Arabian souk, this complex is a rabbit's warren of tiny souvenir stores, bigger shops and more than 50 bars and restaurants, many of which sit right next to the waterways and enjoy spectacular views of the Burj Al Arab. You'll also find The First Group Theatre here, which is a popular venue for plays, musicals and comedy performances throughout the year.

sensasia
urban spa

MASSAGING
Dubai better everyday

MALL OF THE EMIRATES
SensAsia Express
Near Pullman Hotel
t. (9714) 354 9228

THE PALM JUMEIRAH
Shoreline Beach Club 1
Al Nafura
t. (9714) 422 7115

THE VILLAGE
Jumeirah Beach Road
t. (9714) 349 8850

EMIRATES GOLF CLUB
Sheikh Zayed Road
(9714) 417 9820

www.sensasiaspas.com

Spas

Talise Ottoman Spa

Spas
Introduction

Luxurious pampering and Dubai go together like strawberries and cream, or the desert and camels, and you'll find spas of all sizes and styles ready to rub, scrub and knead you into relaxation.

Whether you've just arrived and are in need of a long, lazy day of pampering to help ease you into your vacation, or you have a specific knot that needs to be worked out, someone, somewhere in Dubai will have the necessary facilities and skills to have you feeling better in no time. Pampering is big business here, from the cavernous spas of the biggest hotels to the beautifying villas along Beach Road in Jumeirah, plus all the smaller, boutique massage centres dotted throughout the city.

There are also numerous massage and relaxation techniques available, with prices and standards varying. The opulent 'seven-star' hotels will obviously customise every detail for a blissful experience – and a massage at these usually means you can wallow in Jacuzzis, saunas and steam rooms before and after your treatment – but you'll pay top dollar. Meanwhile, there are plenty of independent places that offer better value for money, but you will have to forego some of the most luxurious facilities. Plenty of hotels have spas pitched somewhere in the middle too.

For a typically Arabian pampering experience, opt for an Oriental hammam. This treatment is traditional in the Middle East region and shares similarities with Turkish baths. The name refers to the bath (the room) in which the treatment takes place – typically an elaborate affair in Dubai's five-star spa scene. A hammam involves a variety of different experiences, including being bathed, scrubbed and massaged on a hot table. It's an absolute must-do and the hammams at The Spa at Jebel Ali Golf Resort & Spa (jebelali-international. com) and Oriental Hammam (royalmirage.oneandonlyresorts. com) are highly recommended, while Jumeirah Zabeel Saray (p.118) has one of the biggest hammams in the Middle East.

A number of spas have couples' treatment rooms where you and your significant other can enjoy a massage at the same time or, if you're the demanding type, you could even opt for a four hands massage.

For a truly unique Dubai memory, try something a little unusual. Assawan at the Burj Al Arab (p.116) offers a caviar body treatment while, not wishing to be left behind, The Ritz-Carlton's spa (ritzcarlton.com) offers a gold leaf body treatment. Finally, for the brave, you can get indulge in a placenta facial at Biolite Skin Clinic (biolitedubai.com).

Relaxing Prices

Certain spas will offer special treatments at certain times of year, as well as reductions on treatments or packages. If you're thinking about indulging yourself, it could also be worth checking out sites like Groupon.com, which often has discounts on spa treatments.

O1

B/Attitude Spa

Location Grosvenor House **Web** grosvenorhouse-dubai.com
Tel 04 399 8888 **Times** 06:00-22:30 (daily)
Map 1 p.211

You could be forgiven for thinking you'd ventured into the Grosvenor House's Buddha Bar (p.80) as you step into the dimly-lit Asian-inspired lobby of B/Attitude. The connection to the spa's sister venue in the neighbouring Grosvenor Tower 1 is obvious – dark colours set the mood and soothing tunes flow. As you sink into the plush, velvety cushions in the relaxation area, you know that you're in for some high-brow designer pampering. Treatments range from the more traditional Eastern massages to Ayurvedic facials and exotic body wraps. Swiss Bellefontaine treatments are also available, but the overall vibe is decidedly Oriental chic – think Tibetan relaxation techniques, sacred stones and Ayurveda, all delivered in impressive treatment rooms that are named after the chakras. There are separate spaces for men and women and the spa boasts 12 treatment rooms in total, as well as two hammam treatment rooms. After a spot of Oriental pampering, pop over to the stunning communal areas which boast saunas, steam rooms, Jacuzzis, hammam pools and an ice fountain, as well as a relaxation area with a juice bar.

Special treatment packages, such as the Oriental Beauty and the Tibetan Magic, often appear on the B/Attitude website and are well worth keeping an eye out for.

02

Cleopatra's Spa & Wellness

Location Wafi **Web**
pyramidsrestaurantsatwafi.com
Tel 04 324 7700 **Times**
09:00-21:00 (daily)
Map 2 p.218

This is an ancient Egyptian affair, with
drapes, silk cushions and majlis-style
seats in the relaxation areas, while the
treatment rooms are comfortable and
softly lit. The spa has a small plunge
pool as well as a Jacuzzi and a sauna.
The menu should satisfy all, with
everything from massages (including
a special pregnancy massage) and
facials to body wraps and anti-ageing
miracles. If you book a spa package,
you get a complimentary pool pass
that grants access to the idyllic tree-
shaded pool area and lazy river.

03

ShuiQi Spa & Fitness

Location Atlantis The Palm **Web** atlantisthepalm.com
Tel 04 426 1020 **Times** 10:00-22:00 (daily)
Map 3 Overview Map

You'll enter this spectacular spa with the highest of expectations and disappointment is definitely not on the menu: from the minute you walk into the boutique area, filled with special beautifying and relaxing goodies to take home, until the end of your treatment, when you'll find yourself smiling through sips of green tea in the relaxation lounge, it's a heavenly experience. Even though this spa has 27 treatment rooms, set over two floors, the beauty of ShuiQi is that it doesn't feel like a big spa; perhaps because of the personal touch that accompanies all treatments, no matter how big or small. Whether you choose a massage, a facial, a Bastien Gonzalez manicure or pedicure, or a four-hour Japanese ritual Shiseido spa journey, your therapist has one clear focus: you. For the ultimate in indulgence, book yourself in for the whole day – the therapists can design a range of treatments individual to you and your requirements.

O4
Armani/Spa

الماء
Acqua

Location Armani Hotel Dubai **Web** dubai.armanihotels.com
Tel 04 888 3888 **Times** 09:00-21:00 (daily)
Map 4 p.216

In keeping with the hotel (p.110) and its Burj Khalifa location, Armani/ Spa is the last word in modern, sleek and elegant design. The space is unusual, with long corridors and multiple doors, which somehow just add to the exclusivity, while the decor follows Armani's famous less is more aesthetic. In fact, while women will certainly enjoy the pampering, the design gives this spa an air of robustness that may appeal more to men than the average candle-scented spa. Within the maze-like infrastructure, there is a sauna, steam and shower rooms offering innovative experiences, as well as the graceful treatment rooms where massages, facials and body wraps fall into one of three categories: Stillness (relaxing), Freedom (rejuvenating), and Fluidity (detoxifying), with a special 'travel recovery' treatment ideal to greet weary new arrivals. The treatment rooms are pod-like and create a real feeling of total disconnection from the outside world – perfect for floating off as you enjoy your delightfully relaxing treatment.

So wide-reaching is the range of the Armani brand, most of the creams, potions and lotions used during treatments here are Armani too, and available to purchase.

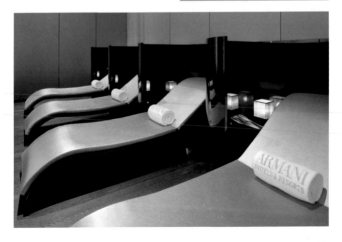

Amara Spa

Location Park Hyatt Dubai **Web** dubai.park.hyatt.com
Tel 04 602 1234 **Times** 10:00-20:00 (daily)
Map 5 p.218

Amara feels like something of a breath of fresh air in Dubai's spa world which, while sublime, can tend to follow the

same formula, making it hard to tell one from another. What sets Amara apart are the treatment rooms. After arriving, guests are escorted directly to the treatment room which acts as a personal spa suite for the entire duration of your visit to the spa. Here, you have all the facilities of a changing room as well as a 'relaxation corner'. After your treatment – or indeed during if you are having a scrub or wrap – you can treat yourself to a shower under the bright Dubai sun in your very own private outdoor shower (very liberating) with a relaxation area for you to dry off under the warm rays. The two-hour Spirit of Amara package is the signature treatment here, involving a scrub with an ancient soap recipe and a rain shower before a full-body aromatherapy massage.

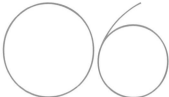

1847

Location Grosvenor House
Web thegroomingco.com
Tel 04 399 8989 **Times** 09:00-
22:00 (daily) **Map** 6 p.211

If 1847 looks more like a gentlemen's club than a spa, that's because men are the centre of attention here. In fact, 1847 was the first dedicated 'grooming lounge' for men to open in the Middle East, although a couple of others have followed suit. Skilled therapists offer traditional grooming, such as shaves, beard styling, facials and hair cuts, while there are other more opulent treatments on offer, such as executive massages, manicures and pedicures. Whether you're looking for relaxation, invigoration or a regular spruce-up, there's something on the menu for you. Other branches are located on The Walk at JBR (04 437 0252), Mirdif City Centre (04 284 034) and Boulevard at Jumeirah Emirates Towers (04 330 1847).

For men in need of pampering, there are a number of other male spas specialising in manly treatments: try Cool Aroma Gents Spa (cool-aroma. com), Urban Male Lounge (nstyleintl.com/uml) and Man/Age (managespa.com). SensAsia Urban Spa (p.133) has a branch at Emirates Golf Club (p.181) which offers a range of treatments tailored specifically to golfers.

07

Talise Spa

Location Boulevard at Jumeirah Emirates Towers **Web** jumeirah.com
Tel 04 319 8181 **Times** 09:00-23:00 (daily)
Map 7 p.217

This regal spa feels like a luxurious coddling getaway, as it is made up of luxurious lounges and treatment rooms that are all connected by garden walkways. The rooms are exotic and well-appointed, with warm shades and ambient music, but it is the welcoming staff that really set this spot apart. They advise on products and technique before your tailored treatment. The range of therapies is extensive but not overwhelming, with a focus on the use of natural oils. A real destination spa, take advantage of the steam room, sauna and plunge pools before or after your appointment, or read a magazine while sipping on ginger tea sweetened with honey in one of the chill out rooms. For a truly exotic experience, you can even opt for your massage to take place outside amongst the gardens.

Talise Spa also organises outdoor yoga sessions, including the extremely popular evening class, which is held on the beach and beneath the stars.

SensAsia Urban Spa

Location The Village **Web** sensasiaspas.com
Tel 04 349 8850 **Times** 10:00-22:00 (daily)
Map 8 p.211, 217

SensAsia may not have all the trimmings of some five-star spas, but the difference is exactly what makes this spa so special. Plus, what it lacks in the way of plunge pools and Jacuzzis, it more than makes up for with the sixty-odd minutes of heightened bliss that spa-goers experience every visit. The hot stone massage, in particular, is sensational, with your choice of aroma, strength of massage and the temperature control of the stones. With treatments from Bali, Thailand and Japan, and prices that undercut the big spas, you'll want to make space in your itinerary for this spa. The relaxation areas, showers and treatment rooms are nonetheless of a very high standard. There are some excellently male-specific treatments too, with sporty types particularly well catered for at the Emirates Golf Club branch.

09

Talise Ottoman Spa

Location Jumeirah Zabeel Saray **Web** jumeirah.com
Tel 04 453 0456 **Times** 09:00-21:00 (daily)
Map 9 p.211

Wandering through the Talise Ottoman Spa, you soon realise that the Zabeel Saray hotel was actually built around this giant spa, rather than vice-versa, such is the central role the spa plays within the resort. With 50 treatment rooms, mineral pools, majlis areas, saunas, ice chambers, couples' suites, gyms and stunning hammams, the spa lays claim to being the biggest in the Middle East and one of the largest in the world. A perfect reconstruction of an opulent Ottoman palace, it's undoubtedly also one of the most luxurious. Men's and women's areas

are apart, each boasting a full set of facilities and treatments – from Thai massage in an outdoor cabana to a complete hydrotherapy journey. But it's the traditional hammam, offering the most authentic Turkish experience in the UAE, that should absolutely not be missed. Prices are at the higher end of the spectrum, of course, but the early bird offer (25% off between 09:00 and 11:00) and VIP/couples' suites (which can be hired by the hour and include treatments) provide somewhat less spendy options. If you're going to splash out once, this is where to do it

10

Angsana Spa
Arabian Ranches

Location Dubai Polo & Equestrian Club **Web** angsanaspa.com
Tel 04 361 8251 **Times** 10:00-21:00 (daily)
Map 10 p.220

The minimalist Asian surroundings feature rich, dark wood, while incense, exotic oils, low lights and soft music set the tone for relaxation. All this may describe half the spas in Dubai and be anything but unique to Angsana, but the quality of the treatments and expertise of the therapists help this spa to stand out from the crowd. The impeccably trained staff work wonders on stressed, aching bodies, turning tight muscles into putty and sending overworked minds to cloud nine. Various styles of treatments are available but the unique massages,

which range from Balinese to Hawaiian to Thai in style, are particularly hard to beat. Angsana is at the higher end of the scale in terms of price, but the quality of treatment is stellar. The Singaporean and Thai Angsana brand is, after all, an affiliate of Banyan Tree which has become a byword for high-end spa opulence. The company has certainly brought its highly reputed standards to its Dubai offerings. Other locations include Dubai Marina (04 368 4356), Emirates Living (04 368 3222) and The Address Montgomerie Dubai (04 360 9322).

Adrenaline Activities

SkyDive Dubai

Adrenaline Activities
Introduction

When it comes to living the ultimate adventure, Dubai is the GCC region's top destination for explorers thanks to the huge number of experiences on offer .

As ever-increasing tourist numbers demonstrate, Dubai's appeal is booming with visitors from all over the world stopping in on the emirate to experience just some of what it has to offer. While giant malls, breathtaking hotels and gravity-defying buildings may be what many expect when they board the plane, more and more are making for Dubai – and, indeed, the rest of the UAE – to experience some incredible activities and unique experiences. From watersports to motorsports, the choice is endless.

Where some see a vast and hypnotic desert, Dubai sees the world's largest adventure playground, offering sensational experiences like dune bashing (p.149), sand boarding and quad biking, as well as camping and horse or camel rides. One of the best ways to experience a variety of these is on an evening or overnight desert safari (p.178).

To really take in the majesty of the desert, those with a head for heights might like to take to the skies. An early morning hot air balloon ride (p.140) is one enthralling way of doing so, while you can also jump into a small plane to be given a bird's eye tour (p.150) of this skyscraper city. The truly intrepid, however, will prefer to jump out of a small plane and parachute down over Palm Jumeirah (p.143).

Aside from the desert and the skies, Dubai's waters also have much to excite thrill-seekers, with activities that range from scuba and boat trips (p.156) to high-octane watersports; there are a number of watersports centres such as Watercooled Dubai (watercooleddubai.com) and Sky & Sea Adventure (watersportsdubai.com) that provide the full gamut of water-based activities, but you'll also find activity providers at the majority of beachfront hotels.

Outside the city, there's plenty to enjoy too with the rest of the emirate rich in outdoor attractions, such as mountain biking, hiking and climbing. Hatta (p.202), which lies an hour to the east, is arguably the emirate's hub for rousing outdoor pursuits but step outside of Dubai (p.188) and you'll find all manner of landscapes that are ripe for discovering, from the tranquil dunes of the Rub' Al Khali to the south, to the majestic peaks of the Hajar Mountains and Musandam to the north.

As if all this wasn't enough, there are also the myriad indoor attractions, climbing walls, simulators and motorsports that are scattered throughout the city and its surroundings. Plenty, then, to keep even the most ardent adrenaline junkie busy during their visit to Dubai.

Man-made Wonders

Dubai's man-made islands – Palm Jumeirah and The World in particular – are world famous. Take your adrenaline trip to the skies to get a unique view of the Dubai shoreline.

O1
Hot Air Balloon

Location various **Web** ballooning.ae, amigos-balloons.com
Tel 02 285 4949, 04 289 9295 **Times** Leaves approx 05:00-06:00 (daily)
Price Guide Dhs.950 (per person)

With its soaring skyscrapers, rolling dunes and spectacular man-made islands, the UAE from the air is an impressive sight. And there's nothing better than taking in the serenity of the desert from a graceful hot air balloon flight. Balloon Adventures organises tours, with flights departing before sunrise. All trips are followed by dune driving.

With Amigos Balloons, you can take a dawn flight over the desert near Fossil Rock and watch the sun rise over the sands. Wear comfortable loose clothing and it's advisable to carry a light jacket or cardigan (ladies, as you will have to climb in and out of the basket, wearing a skirt or heels can be inconvenient). A sun hat or cap is also a good idea.

02
Dubai Autodrome

Location Dubai Motor City **Web** dubaiautodrome.com
Tel 04 367 8700 **Times** 09:00-00:00 **Price Guide** Dhs.600-950 (car),
Dhs.400-850 (motorcycle), Dhs.110 for 15mins karting
Map 2 p.220

Ever dreamed of racing alongside Vettel or flying past Alonso on the last bend of a Formula 1 Grand Prix? The F1-style single-seater experience gets you pretty close. The Dubai Autodrome offers you the opportunity to strap yourself in for a thrilling race around the track. After being given a briefing by the fully-qualified instructors, you'll take to the track fully in charge of the 180bhp Single Seater. The Kartdrome offers a fleet of leisure karts that also deliver an excellent racing experience and has both indoor and outdoor karting areas – the 1.2km international standard circuit features no fewer than 17 corners to test the driver's skills, plus a tunnel and bridge to add to the excitement.

For a great day out of Dubai, head to Yas Island which is on the Dubai side of Abu Dhabi. There, you can experience similar track days on the phenomenal Yas Marina F1 circuit before heading to the Ferrari World themepark.

Jetskiing

Location Ghantoot **Web** jetskidubai.com
Tel 052 983 8959 **Times** 08:30-19:00 (daily)
Price Guide Dhs.250-450 (20 mins to an hour) **Map** **3** p.209

In Dubai, everyone (tourists included) must have a licence to drive a jetski and, therefore, you can't actually rent a jetski within the city itself, but that doesn't mean you have to turn your back completely on high-speed open water fun. In spite of its name, Jet Ski Dubai is actually located just on the Abu Dhabi side of the border in Ghantoot, around 20 minutes drive from Dubai Marina. Jet Ski Dubai rents out jetskis and Ghantoot is a great, safe area to ride; there's a wide manmade channel there that runs around four kilometres from the Golden Tulip and Cassells hotels, right down to the sea. The channel is almost always quiet, giving jetskiers a free run

to pick up some speed and play in each other's wake. At the other end of the city is Al Mamzar Beach Park which sits on the border with Sharjah, just a few minutes' drive from Deira. Here, there are a number of tour operators that rent out jetskis and, being officially in Sharjah, there's no need for a licence. Again, there are channels and lagoons to explore while, as long as you stay clear of the swimming beaches, you can head out a little along the coastline or even check out parts of the under-construction Palm Deira too. For those keen to watch jetskiing in all its glory, the UAE International Jet Ski Championships (dimc.ae) take place every January.

SkyDive Dubai

Location Palm Jumeirah and Al Ain Road **Web** skydivedubai.ae
Tel 050 153 3222 **Times** Dependent on weather
Price Guide Dhs.1,750 **Map** 4 p.211, 209

For the ultimate in adrenaline experiences, it doesn't get more exciting – or maybe just plain scary – than a UAE skydive. Whereas in most of the rest of the world, doing a skydive involves landing in a remote field in the middle of nowhere, in Dubai, you're right in the thick of the action. This is not one for the faint hearted, but if jumping out of a plane to catch views of The Palm Jumeirah is your idea of fun, then head to SkyDive Dubai. The centre is the largest in the Middle East, featuring state-of-the-art equipment and facilities, a location offering superb jumping weather and fully qualified staff. In fact, it is an all-turbine dropzone, meaning that you can expect to jump out of two of the cleanest twin otters in the industry, or an immaculate Pilatus Porter. First-timers can sign up for the tandem jump, where skydivers are attached to a qualified instructor, and prices include digital stills and a DVD of the experience.

UAE experience provider Dreamdays (dreamdays. ae) also organises skydiving experiences. As with SkyDive Dubai, supervised tandem jumps take place along with an experienced professional.

Ski Dubai

Location Mall of the Emirates **Web** theplaymania.com
Tel 800 386 **Times** 10:00-23:00 (Sunday to Wednesday),
10:00-00:00 (Thursday), 09:00-00:00 (Friday), 09:00-11:00 (Saturday)
Price Guide Dhs.180 (2 hour slope pass), Dhs.220 (90 minute lessons)
Map 5 p.213

Some Dubai experiences defy belief.
While temperatures soar outside, you
can find yourself ploughing through
freshly-fallen powder! Ski Dubai
is an indoor ski resort, with more
than 22,500 square metres of 'real'
snow that actually falls from the roof
every night. The temperature hovers
around -3℃, even when it's closer to
40℃ outside, to make for a cooling
excursion from city life. The venue has
five runs that vary in difficulty, height
and gradient, the longest run being
400 metres and falling over 60 metres.
Competent skiers and boarders can
test their skills on the black run, while
beginners can opt for lessons.

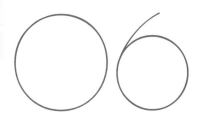

Yellow Boats

Location Dubai Marina **Web** theyellowboats.com
Tel 800 8044 **Times** 10:30-20:00 (daily)
Price Guide Dhs.200 **Map** **6** p.211

If you're after an adrenaline rush on the waters of the Gulf, sign up for a turbo jet experience with The Yellow Boats. These guys offer exhilaratingly fast-paced tours on board eco-friendly inflatable crafts, which allow you to take in some of the best sights of the Arabian Gulf at heart-stopping speeds. After heading out from Dubai Marina and gently cruising past the skyscrapers of the marina and JBR, the captain lets rip and the boat flies over the water past Dubai icons like Palm Jumeirah, Atlantis, the Madinat complex and, finally, Burj Al Arab, twisting and turning along the way. Brace yourself, as you're bound to get a little wet, although the captains do stop at the major landmarks for you to take a few holiday snaps.

As well as the Dubai Marina tour, The Yellow Boats does a high-speed tour of Abu Dhabi Corniche, if you find yourself in need of an adrenaline fix while visiting the capital.

07

Aquarium Dive

Location The Dubai Mall **Web** thedubaiaquarium.com
Tel 04 448 5200 **Times** 10:00-22:00 (Sunday to Wednesday),
10:00-00:00 (Thursday to Saturday)
Price Guide Dhs.1,875 **Map** 7 p.216

Have you ever thought about coming face-to-face with the world's ultimate predator? What would you do if you found yourself nose-to-nose with 10,000 pounds of lean muscle and 10,000 razor-sharp teeth? To find out exactly how you'd react, but without the risk of being mistaken for food, try the Shark Dive at Dubai Aquarium & Underwater Zoo? Whether you are an experienced, certified diver, have never dived before, or do not even know how to swim, you can submerge into the depths of the aquarium's 10-million litre tank and interact with the largest collection of sand tiger sharks in the world. Three shark dives are held each day (each time slot allows for up to four divers), with a dive master and dive instructor supervising every dive, so you'll never feel out of your depth. A number of other diving experiences are also available in the giant aquarium.

08

Surfing

Web surfingdubai.com; surfschooluae.com
Price Guide Dhs.75 per lesson
Map 8 p.213

Dubai is not exactly Surfer's Paradise but, if you're a beginner, the manageable waves and year-round warm water make it a great location to pick up the sport of surfing. There's an enthusiastic community of local surfers to turn to for lessons; if you're already an accomplished surfer, then just check swell alerts through Surf Dubai to find out when the waves are coming in. Sunset Beach (Umm Suqeim Open Beach) is a popular beach, with smallish but decent waves, while the beach off JBR, between the Hilton and Sheraton in Dubai Marina, also sees some waves. Surf Dubai runs 60 to 90 minute group sessions for beginner and intermediate surfers on Sunset Beach and there are also sessions dedicated to kids. Surf School UAE is also a popular option for lessons, owned and managed by keen and experienced surfers.

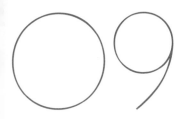

09

Dune Bashing

Location various

If one activity sums up Dubai, it has to be dune bashing. Head out of town in just about any direction at the weekend, and you'll find scores of locals lined up in their 4WDs about to head off on desert-driving adventures. And it's so much fun that both expats and tourists have quickly got in on the act. For most visitors, the best way to experience a spot of dune bashing is on a desert safari (p.178). The experienced driver will amaze you with just what a vehicle is capable of, rocking, rolling, swaying and surfing over the dunes in what is effectively a white-knuckle rollercoaster ride but without the rails. Unfortunately, you can't just rent a 4WD and give it a go yourself as insurance doesn't cover off-road accidents.

If you don't want to rent a 4WD, you can try your hand at quad biking. Many desert safaris offer quadding, while all the main tour operators can also organise a quad bike tour of the nearby desert.

10
Seawings

Location Jebel Ali Golf Resort & Spa **Web** seawings.ae
Tel 04 807 0708 **Times** various
Price Guide From Dhs.695 per person **Map** 10 p.209

It may only be for the most stout-hearted of tourists, but there's no denying that flying is one of the best ways to soak up the awe-inspiring skyline that Dubai has become famous for. The Seawings silver package is a 40-minute dock-to-dock seaplane tour that starts in Jebel Ali and flies across the whole of the city, providing views of Dubai's most iconic landmarks, including the Palm Jumeirah, Burj Khalifa, the World Islands, Burj Al Arab, Dubai Creek and Port Rashid before making a splash landing in Dubai Creek. It's an absolutely stunning experience and one you won't forget in a hurry. Other options include the Burj and Elements packages, which offer just as many highlights. Helicopter tours are increasingly popular too and Aerogulf Services Company (aerogulfservices.com) provides 30 minute chopper tours over Dubai and its main landmarks. If you're feeling extravagant, you can charter a seaplane or helicopter and its captain by the hour and set out your own dream route.

Places In The Sun

Jumeira Open Beach

Places in the Sun
Introduction

Dubai is not short of places for beachgoers to top up their tan or outdoor enthusiasts to enjoy the year-round sunshine. Beaches, parks and plenty more besides...

During the cooler months, there are some excellent outdoor options to discover across Dubai. In fact, there are so many alfresco delights, you might be tempted to never step inside a mall or a hotel during the winter. Dubai's green parks are superbly maintained, while the beaches draw crowds of sunbathers and swimmers, particularly at weekends. But that's not all; there's plenty of fun to be had beyond the city limits too. And, even though you're unlikely to tire of enjoying the urban attractions, there are a couple of huge adventure playgrounds – in the form of the desert and the Arabian Gulf – just waiting to be explored.

There's no doubt that Dubai's beaches are one of the main attractions for visitors. Blessed with warm weather, calm ocean waters and long stretches of sand, the emirate's beaches come in various types, depending on requirement. Choose from public beaches (limited facilities but no entry fee), beach parks (good facilities and a nominal entrance fee), or private beaches (normally part of a hotel or resort). Regulations for public beaches are quite strict, but that's not necessarily a bad thing. Dogs are banned, for instance, and so is driving, therefore the sand is kept clean. Other off-limit activities include barbecues, camping without a permit and holding large parties.

Dubai is also home to a number of excellent parks, with lush green lawns and a variety of trees and shrubs creating the perfect escape from the concrete jungle of the city. Most have a kiosk or cafe selling snacks and drinks, and some have barbecue pits. Remember, these get particularly busy over the weekend.

Regulations at parks vary, with some banning bikes and rollerblades, or limiting ball games to specific areas. Some parks have a ladies' day when entry is restricted to women, girls and young boys.

What not to wear

Compared to the rest of the GCC, Dubai is a fairly liberal city that adopts a much more relaxed attitude to what visitors can wear in public. However, there are some rules that apply to dress and beachwear that visitors must follow. Bikinis are fine in private hotel resorts, although string bottoms and going topless is a big no-no – wherever you are in Dubai. While plenty of beachgoers wear bikinis on public beaches, it can occasionally attract unwanted attention, so best to wear a one piece or sarong while sunbathing or head for a beach park or resort beach. For men, it is worth remembering that some nationalities (and the fashion police) might find Speedos offensive, and avoid going to a nearby cafe or shop without putting a t-shirt on first or you'll be considered rude.

01

Boat Charter

Location Deira, Dubai Marina
Times any
Price Guide varies according to size, number of hours and season
Map 1 p.211, p.218

With a stunning coastline, calm seas and year-round warm waters, a day out on a boat should appear on any explorer's itinerary. There are several options; from a day of sailing around The Palm Jumeirah and along the coast, to an evening's cruise on Dubai Creek or through Dubai Marina – both wonderfully atmospheric. Some companies run regular, scheduled trips on board everything from high-speed RIBs to catamarans with burgers and music on board, while others charter out boats to private parties for sailing or fishing. For something a bit different, head to the Deira side of Dubai Creek where you can find numerous traditional dhows that combine evening sightseeing tours with Arabian cuisine and onboard entertainment. You may even want to look further afield – a dhow cruise in Musandam (known as the Norway of Arabia due to its dramatic coastline) is an unforgettable experience; many operators offer transfers from Dubai. Some offer scuba diving and the option to spend the night on the dhows too.

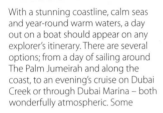

Yachts and catamarans can be chartered from the Dubai Marina area. Try JPS Passenger Yachts (jpsyachts.com) for a range of vessels. One of the most popular charter options is the El Mundo catamaran (elmundodubai.com).

Jumeirah Beach Park

Location Jumeira 2 **Web** definitelydubai.com
Times 07:30-22:00 (Sunday to Wednesday),
07:30-23:00 (Thursday to Saturday)
Price Guide Dhs.5 **Map** **2** p.215

You really get the best of both worlds here with plenty of grassy areas and vast expanses of beach. Facilities include sunbed and parasol hire (Dhs.20 – get there early to ensure they haven't run out), lifeguards, toilets, showers, a couple of snack bars, a play park and numerous barbecue pits. The beach is pristine, the waters are blue and, paddling in the waves and looking back, there's the amazing juxtaposition of the towers of Sheikh Zayed Road climbing above the palm-lined beach. Away from the sandy beach, there are plenty of grassy areas and landscaped gardens which are great for setting up picnics or starting an impromptu game of cricket, football or frisbee. Cycling and rollerblading are not allowed (except for small children). During the cooler months, when it's bearable to get the heart rate up, it's worth venturing onto Jumeira Beach Road for a walk. This road has a laidback holiday vibe to it, with plenty of cafes and restaurants awaiting – just remember to put something on over your swimwear before you head out. Right opposite the Beach Park is Chili's restaurant, with the Lebanese cafe Shu also situated nearby (popular with shisha lovers). Another popular local spot is Beach Park Plaza Centre.

03

Jumeira Open Beach

Location Jumeirah 1
Map 3 p217

Also known as Jumeira Public Beach – or as Russian Beach due to the place's popularity with Russian tourists – Jumeira Open Beach is located next to the Dubai Marine Beach Resort & Spa and Palm Strip Mall. Suitable for soaking up the sun, swimming and people watching, the public beach has lifeguards, shower and bathroom facilities. A good mix of foreign and local beach dwellers take advantage of the sand, water and nearby jogging track. There are a few places to grab snacks and drinks too. It's worth noting though that on Fridays it can get crowded with male visitors, so heading there in a bikini may not be a good idea.

04

JBR Beach

Location Dubai Marina
Map 4 p.211

Previously home to just a handful of waterfront hotels, the Marina is the epitome of new Dubai's rise to modern prominence. Apartment buildings have sprouted up along every inch of the man-made waterway, while between the marina and the shore is the massive Jumeirah Beach Residence (JBR) development, which now dwarfs the five-star beach resorts such as the Hilton and Ritz-Carlton. Just off The Walk at JBR is a decent public beach which is popular during the cooler months. The spaces in front of the hotels are reserved for guests, but there are plenty of areas in between that fill with crowds of families and groups of friends at weekends. The waters are fairly calm here and the shallow areas are scattered with bathers, while the hotels offer a variety of watersports that anyone can sign up for and beach bars to pop into for food or refreshment. Take care when swimming as the public areas usually have no lifeguards; strong rip tides can carry the most confident swimmer away from the shore very quickly.

Located opposite the beach is The Walk at JBR, which has become a huge leisure-time draw for residents and visitors. Strolling from one end to the other of this 1.7km promenade will take you past a whole host of retail and alfresco dining options.

Creek Park

Location Umm Hurair 2 **Web** definitelydubai.com
Tel 04 336 7633 **Times** 08:00-23:30 (daily)
Price Guide Dhs.5 **Map** 5 p.218

Located in the heart of the city, but blessed with acres of lush gardens, fishing piers, jogging tracks, barbecue sites, children's play areas, mini-golf, restaurants and kiosks, Dubai Creek Park is the ultimate in Middle Eastern park life. Four-wheel cycles can be hired from Gate Two for Dhs.20 per hour, while rollerblading is also permitted within the park. Additionally, there's a large amphitheatre, plus the Dubai Dolphinarium (p.42) which runs a popular dolphin and seal show. The park is where you will also find Children's City, an educational project that offers kids their own learning zone and amusement facilities. There's a planetarium focusing on the solar system and space exploration, a nature centre for information on land and sea environments, and the Discovery Space, which reveals the mysteries of the human body.

Running along the park's 2.5km creekfront stretch is a cable car system which allows visitors an unrestricted view of Dubai Creek from 30 metres up in the air.

06
The Desert

With vast areas of virtually untouched wilderness right the way across the UAE, taking to the desert is a very popular pastime. Every other vehicle on the road in Dubai seems to be a 4WD but, unlike in many countries where they're reserved for running the kids to school, there's ample opportunity to truly put them to the off-road test in Dubai. Dune bashing, or desert driving, is one of the toughest challenges for both car and driver, but once you have mastered it, it's also the most fun. Those that want to drive themselves should do so in a controlled environment. OffRoad-Zone (offroad-zone.com) runs a driving centre at the Jebel Ali Shooting Club where you can practise tackling all manner of obstacles. If you don't quite know where to start or don't want to drive yourself then it's worth contacting one of the emirate's many tour companies that offer desert and mountain safari experiences (p.178). These desert safaris are great ways to spend time out in the sands – daytime safaris combine dune bashing with quad biking, camel riding and lunch, while the evening safaris add huge buffets and traditional entertainment to the mix. Some even allow you to camp out under the stars.

Al Safa Park

Location Al Wasl **Web** definitelydubai.com
Tel 04 349 2111 **Times** 08:00-23:00 (daily)
Price Guide Dhs.3 **Map** 7 p.215

This huge, artistically landscaped park is a great place to escape the commotion of nearby Sheikh Zayed Road. Its many sports fields, barbecue sites, play areas and fun fairground rides make it one of the best places in the city to witness the coming together of locals and expats. There's a large boating lake in the centre of the park, tennis and basketball courts for the public, and a flea market (second-hand item sale) held on the first Saturday of every month during the winter. Various informal football and cricket games take place on the large areas of grass. Tuesday is ladies' day, but there is also a permanent ladies' garden within the park. For the health conscious, bikes are available for hire, plus there's a great running track around the park's perimeter that's free of charge to use.

Picnics are a fun and cheap way to spend a lazy afternoon with family or friends. There are Union Co-op and Choithrams supermarkets right next to the park, where you can pick up your lunch. Can't be bothered to shop? There's also a McDonald's and Lebanese bakery nearby!

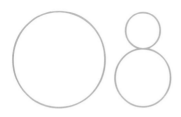

Al Mamzar Park

Location Al Mamzar **Web** definitelydubai.com
Tel 04 296 6201 **Times** 08:00-23:00 (daily)
Price Guide Dhs.5 (per person), Dhs.30 (per car) **Map** 8 p.219

With its four clean beaches, open spaces and plenty of greenery, Al Mamzar Park and the Beach Park are popular spots – although the previously clear sea views have become a little obstructed by the work on the Palm Deira. Situated at the mouth of Khor al-Mamzar, just across the lagoon from Sharjah, the well-maintained white sandy beaches have sheltered areas for swimming, as well as changing rooms with showers. Lifeguards, meanwhile, are on duty between 08.00 and 18:00 on at least one of the small beaches, and the waters are quite calm. There are also two pools that are monitored by lifeguards throughout the week. To make the most out of your day, air-conditioned chalets, with barbecues, can be rented (ranging from Dhs.150 to Dhs.200). Al Mamzar Beach Park is a particularly suitable location for families with children, as there are plenty of open spaces with play areas, climbing obstacles and a wooden castle. Bikes are also available for hire. To grab a bite to eat, a main restaurant is available in the main park area, complemented by ten snackhouses, scattered around the venue.

> This lush, landscaped park is something of a hidden gem in Dubai and, therefore, is usually quite empty during the week. As with any public park or beach, it can become more crowded with men-only groups on a Friday.

Jebel Ali Golf Resort & Spa

Location Waterfront **Web** jebelali-international.com
Tel 04 814 5555 **Map** 9 p.209

Just far enough out of Dubai to escape the hustle and bustle, the Jebel Ali Golf Resort & Spa offers resplendent surroundings, with a peaceful atmosphere – the perfect place for a weekend break. The two distinct properties, the Jebel Ali Hotel and The Palm Tree Court & Spa, are set in 128 acres of lush, landscaped gardens, with an 800-metre private beach, a marina and a golf course. Guests can also enjoy horse riding and shooting.

One shoreline gem at Jebel Ali Golf Resort & Spa is Watercooled Dubai (watercooleddubai.com). It offers a full range of watersports from SUP, kayaks and sailing to wakeboarding, waterskiing, wakesurfing and kitesurfing. The centre has become a popular hangout for regular watersporters.

Nasimi Beach

Location Atlantis The Palm **Web** atlantisthepalm.com
Tel 04 426 2626 **Times** 09:00-00:30 (Saturday to Thursday),
09:00-02:00 (Friday)
Map 10 Overview Map

Located at Atlantis, The Palm, Nasimi Beach Club boasts a relaxed vibe and, even if you're not staying at the vast resort, you can jump on a day bed (on a first-come-first-serve basis) provided you spend a minimum of Dhs.150 per person on food and beverages. This also gets you free access to the zero-entry swimming pool. Meanwhile, located close to the beach is Nasimi's very own restaurant and bar, where the select menu features expertly prepared seafood and meat dishes. A day out at Nasimi Beach does not come cheap, but it's a great Dubai experience. Although a luxuriously chilled-out place to spend the day, it is as the sun begins to set at the weekend that this stretch of beach really comes to life thanks to a plethora of live events during the winter months. Everyone from the Erykah Badu and Richard Ashcroft, to Example, Snow Patrol, Calvin Harris and The Script have graced the shores of Nasimi Beach during these festivals.

bubbalicious

THE WESTIN BRUNCH
EVERY FRIDAY 1PM - 4PM

"It isn't easy to land the best brunch title but The Westin's bubbalicious has done just that!" - **Aquarius**

"It's official! The best brunch in Dubai is Bubbalicious" - **Ahlan!**

BUBBALICIOUS
Bubbalicious spread with free flow Bubbly
Adult: **590 PP**
Bubbalicious spread with free flow Sparkling
Adult: **490 PP**

DELICIOUS
Bubbalicious spread and soft drinks
Adult: **350 PP** Kids 6 - 12 years: **190 PP** Kids below 6 years: **Free**

• Live Band • Petting Zoo • Chinese Acrobats • Jumping Castle • Kids Gaming Corner
Booking essential - The Westin Dubai Mina Seyahi Beach Resort & Marina- 04 511 7136

Dubai Experiences

Dune Bashing

Dubai
Experiences
Introduction

The once sleepy fishing village has now transformed into a modern metropolis and a 21st century icon. It's an intoxicating place filled with experiences to match.

Many of Dubai's most ambitious projects are now recognised all over the world, from the majestic Burj Al Arab (p.116) and the colossal Burj Khalifa (p.172) to the awesome Palm Jumeirah. Dubai is a byword for luxurious indulgence, multicultural lifestyles, architectural excess, lavish beach holidays and general fun in the sun, but it is also gaining a reputation for being one of the most diverse tourist destinations on the planet; a place where your appetite can be sated, whether you're into relaxed beach holidays, cultural breaks, activity trips or sporting tours.

And while Dubai may be all things to all people, there are a few specific activities and experiences that are either unique to the City of Gold, or perfectly sum up a side of the city. The juxtaposition of old and new, the mix of traditional Arabia with the west, is one characteristic that baffles, intrigues and delights visitors and, with that in mind, the various bus (p.183) and boat tours (p.156) provide the perfect perspective to take in this contrast. Being in a traditional spice souk one moment and a shiny, sprawling mall the next is pure Dubai.

While you're in the mood for touring, then a desert safari (p.178) – which usually comes complete with an Arabian buffet, entertainment and dune bashing – is the kind of experience you'll struggle to find elsewhere; hot air ballooning (p.140)

may be available in other locations, but doing it as the sun rises over the desert is pretty special.

In terms of modern Dubai, you'll want to spend some time in the new Downtown area, which is home to The Dubai Mall (p.92) as well as Souk Al Bahar (p.99) and The Dubai Fountain. But dominating Downtown is, of course, the Burj Khalifa and looking out from the viewing deck of the world's tallest building (p.172) is an experience that is only available in Dubai – until someone builds a bigger tower, of course.

Overindulgence is undeniably a Dubai trait as well, and there's no doubt that residents and visitors in the city like to enjoy the finer things in life. Brunch (p.184) may be available around the world, but the Dubai brunch is something else entirely and a sight to behold – and dive into – while afternoon tea (p.173) in the city has all the old world charm you'd expect to find in London or Paris rather than the Middle East.

Taste of Arabia
Tucking into traditional mezze and grilled meats, washing it all down with a fresh fruit juice and finishing your meal with a shisha pipe may not be unique to Dubai, but it is pure Arabia and Dubai has some of the best places to enjoy that traditional experience.

Observation Deck at Burj Khalifa

Location Burj Khalifa **Web** burjkhalifa.ae
Tel 800 2884 3867 **Times** 10:00-22:00 (Sunday to Wednesday),
10:00-00:00 (Thursday to Saturday)
Price Guide Dhs.100 (if booked in advance) **Map** 1 p.216

The Burj Khalifa finally reached its peak in 2010 when, at over 828 metres in height, it officially became the tallest building on earth – by some distance too. Anyone staying at the plush Armani Hotel Dubai will get to experience the building first-hand; for everyone else, a taste of the views on offer come from visiting At.mosphere (p.58) or heading to At The Top – the 124th floor observation deck that offers staggering 360° views over the whole city, as well as Downtown and The Dubai Fountain far, far below.

The high-speed lifts, which deliver you to At The Top at 40kph, are themselves almost worth the trip alone. There's also information about the Burj and its construction, and a gift shop.

Images courtesy of Emaar Properties

O2 Afternoon Tea

Location various
Times 12:00-17:30 (daily)
Price Guide Dhs.60-Dhs.425

Perhaps it's a throwback to those pre-1971 days when the UAE fell under British rule, or maybe it has something to do with the big, luxurious hotels being eager to bring a little hedonistic extravagance back to a time of the day that is sadly all too often ignored; but, for some reason, you'll find that afternoon tea is a bit of a big deal in Dubai. Whether you opt for a traditional Earl Grey, a camomile, a rooibos, a healthy green tea, or even an exotic fruit tea, it's always served up with delicate sandwiches, fresh scones and clotted cream, and more pastries than you could ever possibly imagine. For a traditional elegance, you really can't beat tea in the lobby lounge at the Ritz-Carlton on JBR; while the Skyview Bar at the Burj Al Arab offers a grand, champagne-backed affair. Try the Sultan's Lounge at Zabeel Saray for afternoon tea with a Turkish twist (followed by a relaxing shisha).

O3
Dubai's Sporting Calendar

Location various
Web dubaicalendar.ae

Dubai is synonymous with beaches, malls and extravagant hotels but, increasingly, the city is gaining a reputation as a first-class sporting destination. Aided by building the best sporting facilities that money can buy, some of the biggest (and biggest money) events in the global calendar have been drawn to Dubai and, as a city that always likes a good knees-up, they're always spectator-friendly, fun events. The year begins with the Dubai Marathon, the Dubai Desert Classic (which has attracted legends like Tiger Woods and Ernie Els) and the Dubai Duty Free Tennis, where Nadal and Federer are quite the regulars. There's the Dubai World Cup – the world's richest horse race – the Dubai World Championship (the finale of the European golf season), and, best of all for Dubai's revellers, the year ends with the Dubai Rugby Sevens – one of the biggest social events in the calendar, attracting more than 100,000 spectators. The city has also seen world championship swimming and diving events, international cricket matches, plus there's a regular calendar of horse racing, polo and off-roading. So, no matter when you visit, there's sure to be an event to catch.

Down the road in Abu Dhabi, even more huge sporting events await, like the F1 Grand Prix, the HSBC Golf Championships, the Mubadala World Tennis Championship and the Abu Dhabi International Triathlon.

Friday Polo at Dubai Equestrian Club

Location Dubai Studio City **Web** poloclubdubai.com
Tel 04 361 8111 **Times** 15:30 (Wednesday, Friday & Saturday)
Price Guide Dhs.50-Dhs.125 **Map** 4 p.220

The Dubai Polo & Equestrian Club stages Friday and Saturday chukka events during the polo season (the cooler winter months) and rather spiffing events they are too. Don't worry if you don't know the first thing about polo – you'll be in good company and you'll soon pick up the rules anyway, but polo events are all about the social aspect anyway. For Dhs.50, you can drive pitchside and set up your picnic chairs and blanket, bringing along a cool box full of the finest fare you could find – it really is the perfect way to while away a sunny afternoon. For a more extravagant option, you can either order a bespoke Polo Picnic Box from the polo clubhouse for Dhs.125 per person, or book a table at the terrace restaurant and watch the action unfold from there. Polo matches start around 15:30 but arrive from 13:30 to get the pick of the parking spots, or better still get a cab there so that you can enjoy mingling with other spectators and players at the polo after-party from 18:00 to midnight. There are a number of major international tournaments throughout the year, with February's Dubai Polo Gold Cup being arguably the pick of them.

05

Dhow Dinner Cruise

Location various
Times 19:30-22:30 (daily)
Price Guide Dhs.120-Dhs.345

One of the Dubai must-do experiences for visitors, dhow dinner tours take place along Dubai Creek and from Dubai Marina at the other end of town. Traditionally trading crafts that ship cargo between the Gulf and Iran, these dhows have been converted to become floating restaurants; the two to three hour tours typically see diners sit on the top deck, beneath the stars, while an Arabian buffet is served up. All the main tour operators offer dhow dinner cruises and which one you pick depends on your preferred backdrop – creek cruises take in the traditional landmarks of Deira and Bur Dubai, while marina cruises reveal the bright lights of modern Dubai and The Palm.

06
Desert Safari

Location various
Times 15:00-21:00 (daily)
Price Guide around Dhs.250 per person

You can go almost anywhere and lie on a beach, laze by the pool, take to the shops and dine at high-end restaurants – what makes a trip to Dubai truly special are the kind of experiences that are totally unique to this region and desert safaris certainly fit that bill. All of the main tour operators offer very similar experiences and you should be able to book directly with your hotel. For the full Arabian experience, book an evening safari – you'll be picked up in a 4WD from your hotel before being whisked away into the desert where your experienced driver will show you exactly what off-road vehicles were made for. After the rollercoaster 4WD ride, you'll stop on one of the tallest dunes to watch the sun go down over the vast desertscape and take your next Facebook profile picture, before you get back into the vehicle to be taken to a Bedouin-style desert camp. There, you can ride a quad bike, mount a camel, have your hands painted with henna, or smoke shisha before the Arabian banquet is brought out and the entertainment – in the form of a belly dancer and a whirling dervish dancer. Finally, it's back to the 4WD for the journey back to your hotel.

Golf on a Championship Course

Location various **Web** dubaigolf.com
Times 06:00-22:00 (daily)
Price Guide Dhs.260-Dhs.695 (18 holes)

With stars like Nick Faldo, Colin Montgomerie, Ernie Els and Ian Baker-Finch all lending their star-power to Dubai's greens through their successful design collaborations, it is little surprise that the popularity of the city as a world-class golf destination has now been cemented. Clubs and societies from all over the world make the golf tour to Dubai an integral part of their annual schedules. Of course, hotels and tour operators can pre-book your tee times if you're heading over for a golf-heavy few days, but Dubai Golf (dubaigolf.com) also operates a central reservation system for those wishing to book a round of golf on any of the major courses in the emirate. Just don't leave it until the actual day you want to play or you may struggle to get a tee time.

Top ten golf courses

Emirates Golf Club Map **11** p.211
dubaigolf.com
Dubai Creek Golf & Yacht Club
Map **12** p.218
dubaigolf.com
Jumeirah Golf Estates
Map **13** Overview Map
jumeirahgolfestates.com
Montgomerie Golf Club Map **14** p.211
themontgomerie.com
The Els Club Map **15** p.220
elsclubdubai.com
Al Badia Golf Club Map **16** p.223
albadiagolfclub.ae
Arabian Ranches Golf Club
Map **17** p.220
arabianranchesgolfdubai.com
Jebel Ali Golf Resort & Spa
Map **18** p.209
jebelali-international.com
Saadiyat Beach Golf Club Map **19** p.208
sbgolfclub.ae
Al Hamra Golf Club Map **20** p.209
alhamragolf.com

You may like to time your golf trip to coincide with the Dubai World Championships which, incredibly, offers free tickets to spectators and is a real hit with fans and merrymakers alike.

Shisha

Location various
Times any time
Price Guide Dhs.50-Dhs.200

Smoking the traditional shisha (water pipe) is a popular pastime enjoyed throughout the Middle East. Also known as hookah or hubbly bubbly, the proper name is argile, and it is usually savoured in a local cafe while chatting with friends. Shisha pipes can be smoked with a variety of aromatic flavours, such as strawberry, grape or apple, and you'll know when you're walking past a shisha cafe thanks to the sweet scent floating on the breeze. The experience is unlike normal cigarette or cigar smoking as the smoke is 'smoothed' by the water, creating a much more soothing effect, although smoking shisha does still cause smoking related health problems. Some of the most popular spots include QD's (p.84), BarZar (p.70) and the terraces at Shakespeare & Co, which has branches in Souk Al Bahar, The Dubai Mall, Emirates Hills, The Village Mall and Arabian Ranches, amongst others. Try the grape with mint for a particularly lovely taste.

Big Bus Tour

Location various **Web** bigbustours.com
Tel 04 340 7709 **Times** 08:00-17:00, 19:00-22:00 (daily)
Price Guide Dhs.220 (adult 24h); Dhs.125 (adult night)

If you only booked a short break in Dubai, or perhaps are stopping in for a few days en route to an even farther-flung destination, then you'll want to see as much of this incredible city as possible in a short amount of time and a bus tour is an excellent option for seeing all the highlights in one go. The Big Bus Tour is arguably the pick of the tours; providing bus tours of 12 cities around the globe, from Budapest to Shanghai, this hop-on hop-off tour knows exactly what tourists want to see from its fleet of double-deckers, as well as just what they want to hear on the commentary track. You can choose between 24 and 48 hour tickets, depending on just how whistle-stop you want

your tour to be. If you have the time, then the 48 hour ticket is definitely worthwhile as it includes free entry to Dubai Museum and Sheikh Saeed Al Maktoum's House, as well as a walking tour of the old town, and trips on a dhow creek cruise and a ride on an RTA water bus; frankly, you'll need two days to fit in all of that little lot.

> The Big Bus Company also runs a two-hour night tour, leaving from either Deira City Centre or Souk Madinat. It's a great way to get a quick overview of the city while enjoying the Dubai sunset.

Friday Brunch

Location various
Times 12:00-16:30
Price Guide Dhs.95-Dhs.695

You might think the word 'brunch' is self-explanatory: a portmanteau of 'breakfast' and 'lunch' – a meal you have between the two more accepted dining anchors. If so, you clearly haven't had brunch in Dubai. It may have been invented in the States, and given kudos in New York, but Dubai has taken the brunch on to a whole new level. Here, it's a hobby, a social skill, a weekend institution, the calorific glue that holds the weekend together. Far from the genteel image of croissants, scrambled eggs and good coffee over the day's newspapers, brunch in Dubai is synonymous with triumphantly eating your own body weight in food and washing it down with free-flowing champagne. And all

for a set price. Waxy's, Double Decker, Spice Island, Warehouse and Yalumba are the spiritual homes of the truly debauched brunch, while Carter's and Mazina are both child-friendly options, offering smaller portions and a less alcohol-orientated atmosphere, and Thai Kitchen, Organic Foods & Café and Zuma (p.62) offer something a bit different. For a taste of brunch, and Dubai, at its most decadent, Spectrum on One epitomises Dubai's posh and pricey all-inclusive approach, inviting diners to feed on the entire world (from Japan to Europe via India), swig from endless champagne flutes, and feel classy while doing it. Al Qasr, Farriers and Armani/Hashi are all equally high-minded affairs.

As well as giant buffets that feature everything from soups and salads to sushi and sashimi, most of the biggest brunches have live cooking stations, where you can choose ingredients and ask chefs to knock up stir-fries, pizzas or pasta dishes.

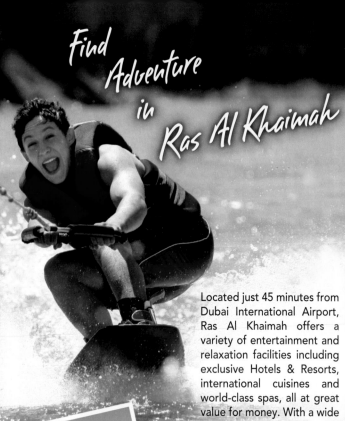

Find Adventure in Ras Al Khaimah

Located just 45 minutes from Dubai International Airport, Ras Al Khaimah offers a variety of entertainment and relaxation facilities including exclusive Hotels & Resorts, international cuisines and world-class spas, all at great value for money. With a wide range of adventure and sports activities covering desert camps, golf courses, watersports and micro light aviation, the emirate of Ras Al Khaimah offers the ultimate outdoor experience.

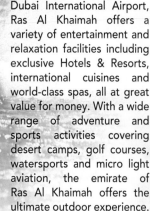

www.rasalkhaimahtourism.com

Ras Al Khaimah
A RISING EMIRATE

Outside Of Dubai

Fujairah

Outside Of Dubai
Introduction

From the vast Rub Al Khali desert in the south, to the majestic Hajar Mountains in the north, there's an incredible country to visit outside of Dubai's city limits.

Dubai may have everything from ski slopes and souks to boutiques and beaches, but there are a number of interesting and varied areas outside of the city borders too: with the other emirates in the UAE, as well the neighbouring country of Oman all warranting exploration, there's plenty to keep you busy.

All six of the other emirates in the UAE – Abu Dhabi, Ajman, Fujairah, Ras Al Khaimah, Sharjah and Umm Al Quwain – are within a two-hour drive of the centre of Dubai. From the sleepy streets of Umm Al Quwain and the rugged mountains of Ras Al Khaimah to the cultural grandiose of Sharjah, each emirate has something different to offer, and each can be explored, at least in part, over a weekend. Abu Dhabi, in particular, should be visited if you have time – even if it's just for an afternoon. The drive takes an hour or two, depending on which part of the capital you're heading to. There are plenty of essential attractions to explore, from Emirates Palace (the world's most expensive hotel) and the delightful Corniche (great for an evening stroll), to the Grand Mosque and the islands that are now being developed into must-visit destinations in their own right. Plus, you'll find some major international sporting events and concerts by musical giants like Prince, Coldplay and Beyonce.

The country's vast deserts and harsh-looking mountains are equally accessible, with a copy of the *UAE Off-Road Explorer*, and can be reached within a 45 minute drive of Dubai, if you need to avoid civilisation for a while. All of the big tour operators offer one to several day excursions into the mountains or desert, including accommodation which ranges from camping to five-star hotels.

There are also several incredible resort hideaways that combine comfortable lodgings with unique activities and these are well worth a weekend, if you're planning on spending a week or two in the UAE.

Dubai's status as an international hub means it's easy to find quick, cheap flights to the neighbouring GCC countries of Oman, Saudi Arabia, Qatar, Bahrain and Kuwait, none of which are more than a 90 minute flight away. Oman, considered by many to be one of the most beautiful and culturally interesting countries in the region, is easily reached and explored by car, with Muscat just a four hour drive from Dubai.

All You Need To Know
In addition to handy visitors' guides like *Dubai Top Ten* and *Dubai Mini Visitors' Guide*, Explorer publishes the fantastic *UAE Off-Road Explorer*, *Oman Off-Road Explorer* and the *Ultimate UAE Explorer* – if you love getting outdoors and active on your holidays, these guides contain everything you need to know. Pick up your copies online from askexplorer.com/shop.

Ras Al Khaimah

Web rasalkhaimahtourism.com
Map 1 p.209

With the Hajar Mountains rising just behind the city, the Arabian Gulf stretching out from the shore and the desert starting in the south near the farms and ghaf forests of Digdagga, Ras Al Khaimah (RAK) has possibly the best scenery of any emirate. A creek divides the main city of the most northerly emirate into the old town and the newer Al Nakheel district. The past couple of years have witnessed RAK's transformation into a prominent weekend destination, and several new resorts have opened. Ras Al Khaimah contains several archaeological sites, some dating back all the way to 3000BC, and if you take the Al Ram road out of the Al Nakheel district and towards the Hajar Mountains, you'll discover some of the area's history, including the Dhayah Fort, Shimal Archaeological Site and Sheba's Palace. Many of the artefacts discovered in these locations can now be found at the National Museum in Ras Al Khaimah city, while the Pearl Excursion and Pearl Museum (rakpearls.com) are reminders of Ras Al Khaimah's more recent heritage and trade.

> The Tower Links Golf Course (towerlinks.com) is laid out among the mangroves around the creek and is popular at weekends, as is Al Hamra Golf Club (alhamragolf.com).

Oman

Web omran.om
Map 2 p.209

The most accessible country from
the UAE, Oman is a peaceful and
breathtaking destination, with history,
culture and spectacular scenery
to spare. The capital, Muscat, has
enough attractions to keep you busy
for a long weekend, with beautiful
beaches, great restaurants and cafes,
the mesmerising old souk at Mutrah,
and the Sultan Qaboos Mosque.
Outside the capital are many historic
towns and forts. You'll also discover
some of the most stunning mountain
and wadi scenery in the Middle East,
while Salalah, deep in the south
of Oman, has the added bonus of
being cool and wet even during
the summer months. The drive from
Dubai to Muscat takes just four hours
and provides some stunning views
en route, or you can hop on a flight
from Dubai to Muscat which takes
just 45 minutes. There is also a bus
service from Dubai to Muscat that
takes around six hours and costs from
Dhs.50 (ontcoman.com).

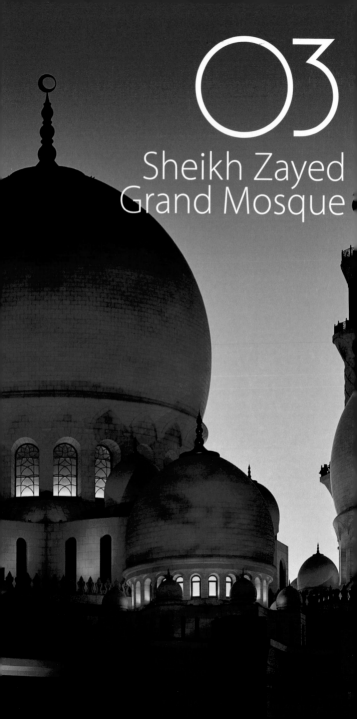

03

Sheikh Zayed
Grand Mosque

Location Al Maqtaa, Abu Dhabi **Web** szgmc.ae
Tel 02 441 6444 **Times** 09:00-22:00 (Saturday to Thursday),
closed Friday mornings
Price Guide Free **Map** 3 p.209

The stunning Sheikh Zayed Grand Mosque opened in 2007, and has captivated worshippers and visitors since. This work of art is the largest mosque in the UAE, and one of the largest in the world, with a capacity for an astonishing 40,000 worshippers, which it often sees during Eid. The Grand Mosque dominates arrival on the island via the Al Maqtaa, Mussafah and Sheikh Zayed Bridges, towering over the south of the island and so white it appears to almost shimmer underneath the clear blue skies. The mosque's first event was the funeral of its namesake, Sheikh Zayed, who is buried at the site. Architecturally, the mosque was inspired by Mughal and Moorish traditions, with classical minarets. The most amazing features are the 80 domes, over 1,000 columns, 24 carat gold-plated chandeliers and the world's largest hand-woven Persian carpet, which was designed by a renowned Iranian artist. If the effect is breathtaking during the day, then words can barely describe the vision that is the Grand Mosque illuminated at night. Unlike other mosques, Sheikh Zayed Mosque is open for non-Muslims to tour between 09:00 and 22:00 every day except for Friday mornings, although you might like to time your visit to coincide with one of the free 'walk in' guided tours that take place at 10:00, 11:00 and 17:00 during the week, at 17:00 and 19:30 on Fridays, and at 10:00, 11:00, 14:00, 17:00 and 19:30 on Saturdays. Not only will you learn more about the Grand Mosque but about Islam in general.

Remember to dress conservatively if you plan to visit the Grand Mosque. Men should avoid wearing shorts or short sleeves, while women should wear loose-fitting clothes that cover legs and shoulders. Shawls are provided at the entrance for ladies to cover their heads.

O4

Dreamland

Location Umm Al Quwain **Web** dreamlanduae.com
Tel 06 768 1888 **Times** 10:00-18:00 (Sunday to Thursday),
10:00-19:00 (Friday & Saturday)
Price Guide Dhs.85 (below 1.2m), Dhs.135 **Map** 4 p.209

The country's original waterpark is
still well worth the trip out of town.
With over 25 water rides, including
four 'twisting dragons', the Twister and
the Kamikaze, Dreamland is massive,
spread across 250,000 square metres of
landscaped gardens that look out over
the beautiful Umm Al Quwain lagoon,
with its mangroves and flamingos.
If extreme slides aren't your thing,
there's the lazy river, a wave pool, an
aqua play area, bumper boats, and
a high-salinity floating pool. In fact,
Dreamland is probably the most child-
friendly of all the UAE's waterparks.
Not that adults are overlooked – in
addition to the usual smattering of
snack bars and restaurants, you'll also
find the country's largest pool bar here.

For a really quirky overnight
experience, you can stay
in cabins or tents within
Dreamland, granting you 36
hour access to the park, as
well as an evening BBQ. You'll
then get breakfast before
hitting the slides again.

Nothing stops you here!

05

Qasr Al Sarab

Location Liwa **Web** anantara.com
Tel 02 886 2088 **Map** 5 p.208

One of the most sensational
wilderness resorts in the world ,
this luxury hotel is an epic citadel
deep in the sand-sea hinterland.
Situated in the astonishing Rub Al
Khali, or Empty Quarter (the world's
largest uninterrupted body of sand),
every aspect of this resort is film-set
spectacular. Walled and turreted, the
main body of the resort is within one
enormous complex, while across the
valley is a luxurious villa compound
popular with VIPs. The incredible spa
is worth the journey here itself, while
the sprawling swimming pool has a
swim-up bar and is surrounded by
tented day beds secreted among the
palm trees.

Al Ain Zoo

Location Zoo District, Al Ain **Web** alainzoo.ae
Tel 800 2977 **Times** 10:00-22:00 (daily),
16:00-22:00 (June to September)
Price Guide Dhs.5 (3-12yrs), Dhs.15 (Adults) **Map** 6 p.209

Stretching over 900 hectares, this is
the largest and best zoo in the region.
With ample greenery, a casual stroll
through the paths that criss-cross the
park makes for a wonderful family day
out. As well as seeing apes, reptiles
and big cats, you can get up close
to local species such as the Arabian
oryx and sand gazelle, or pay a visit
to the fantastic birdhouse. The zoo
is a centre for endangered species'
conservation and visitors can look
forward to spotting true rarities.
Nearly 30% of the 180 species are
endangered and the park is even
home to a stunning pair of white
tigers and white lions. Family nights
with fun activities take place on
Wednesdays. A park train regularly
departs from the central concourse,
providing a whirlwind tour of the zoo.

07

Yas Island

Location Abu Dhabi
Web yasisland.ae
Map 7 p.209

Following Dubai's lead, Abu Dhabi has gone about turning a series of islands into massive leisure destinations in their own right; unlike The Palm or The World, both Saadiyat and Yas are natural islands that have been redeveloped rather than raised from the ocean bed. While Saadiyat's main attractions – local branches of the Louvre and Guggenheim museums along with other museums, concert halls and exhibition centres – are still a few years away, Yas Island is already drawing in the crowds. First and foremost, it's where you'll find the Yas Marina F1 Circuit which, each November, sees the Formula One circus and all its fans come to town. Aside from the F1, there are all manner of track days and karting experiences that you can enjoy all year round. One of the circuit's most iconic elements is the incredible and futuristic Yas Viceroy hotel that spans the track; it is worth a visit at any time of year thanks to the space-age interiors and excellent restaurants you'll find inside, such as Amici and Kazu. Nearby is the marina itself, which is packed full with million dollar leisure yachts, and the exceptional Yas Links golf course, which was created by renowned course designer Kyle Phillips and is the first links course in the Middle East. There are several other hotels, such as the Crowne Plaza, Radisson Blu and Centro, that also back onto the course and offer some great restaurants and bars, as well as lovely pool areas. The main attraction, for the moment at least, must be Ferrari World. The world's biggest indoor theme park is an architectural wonder and a must for any fan of the brand, although even non racing fans will love the rides which include Formula Rossa, the world's fastest rollercoaster.

08

Sharjah

Web sharjahtourism.ae
Map 8 p.209

Sharjah was named the cultural capital of the Arab world by Unesco in 1998, thanks to its eclectic mix of museums, heritage preservation and souks. If you're staying in Dubai, it's an easy day, or even an afternoon trip. The city is built around Khalid Lagoon, and the surrounding Buheirah Corniche is popular for evening strolls. Small dhows can be hired to take you out on the water to see the city lights. Joining Khalid Lagoon to Al Khan Lagoon, Al Qasba is home to a variety of cultural events, theatre and music – all held on the canal-side walkways or at dedicated venues. The biggest and most visible draw is the Eye of the Emirates – a 60m high observation wheel with air-conditioned pods offering amazing views over Sharjah and across to Dubai.

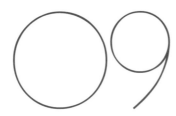

09

Hatta

Web hattaforthotel.com
Tel 04 809 9333
Map 9 p.209

Less than an hour from Dubai, Hatta feels a whole world away, making it a great spot for a break from the hustle and bustle. Outside the town, there are plenty of off-roading opportunities, including the Hatta pools where you can take a cooling dip, whereas, if you prefer your action on two wheels, then this is also a popular area for cyclists. Back in town, the Heritage Village is constructed around an old settlement and was restored in the style of a traditional mountain village. Hatta's history goes back over 3,000 years and the area includes a 200 year-old mosque and a fort, which is now used as a weaponry museum. Hatta Fort Hotel is a secluded retreat featuring 50 chalet-style suites which come with patios overlooking the Hajars and the tranquil gardens; the hotel also doubles as the area's main activity provider, with swimming pools, floodlit tennis courts, mini golf and a driving range, as well as an archery range (instruction is available).

10

Desert Islands

Location Sir Bani Yas Island **Web** desertislands.com
Tel 02 801 5400 **Map** **10** p.208

This private island hideaway, located on Sir Bani Yas Island which was once the private retreat of the great Sheikh Zayed, is accessible only by boat or via the hotel 's private aircraft – retreats don't get much more exclusive than that. The unique resort is a beach hotel and safari lodge rolled into one, and has become a favourite weekend hideaway for the urban elite. The pool, shaded by palm trees and staring out across the beach and sea, is beautiful and inviting. Tented sunloungers and oversized bean bags are dotted around the landscaped grounds. Away from the pool, there are plenty of activities to keep guests entertained. The spa is a sensation, as popular for sociable weekend manicures as for indulgent, individual, massage treatments. Set quietly apart from the main hotel building, it has calm views across the beach to the sea. For the more adventurous, African safari-style jeeps swing up to the hotel entrance just before dawn and dusk each day to take guests to see the island's extraordinary wildlife. Expert guides will take you to find local favourites like oryx and gazelles, as well as all sorts of animals you would never have expected in this part of the world, such as deer, giraffes, cheetahs, hyenas, emus, dolphins and sea turtles. Among the many ways to explore and enjoy the island are kayaking, mountain biking, hiking and snorkelling, while activities such as archery are also available. Back at the hotel, a floodlit tennis court and a comprehensively equipped fitness centre take care of any excess energy.

Sir Bani Yas is the UAE's biggest natural island, lying just nine kilometres offshore. It is one of the Desert Islands – a collection of eight protected islands that are being developed for eco-tourism.

It was the late Sheikh Zayed who turned Sir Bani Yas into Arabia's largest nature reserve as a way of protecting many natural species. The island plays a key role in preservation, with some 10,000 animals a year from Sir Bani Yas being released back into the wild.

unconditional
medical care where needed,
when needed

MSF is an international, independent, medical humanitarian organization that delivers emergency aid to people affected by armed conflict, epidemics, healthcare exclusion and natural disasters. Everyday 27,000 MSF aid workers offer assistance to people based only on need and irrespective of race, religion, gender or political affiliation.

MSF works in over 60 countries around the world.

© Ton Koene. Victims of severe floods in Pakistan (2010).

MEDECINS SANS FRONTIERES
أطبـاء بـلا حـدود

www.msf-me.org
MSF Regional Office +971 2 631 7645 PO Box 47226 Abu Dhabi, UAE

Maps

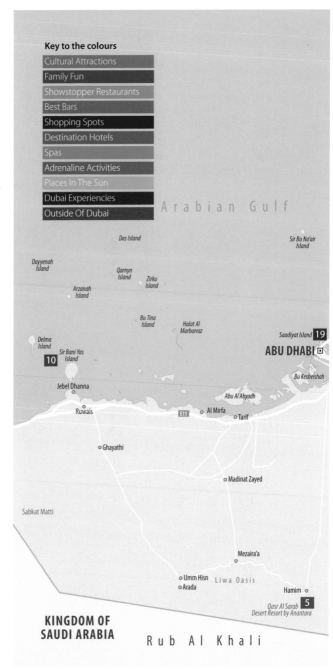

Key to the colours

- Cultural Attractions
- Family Fun
- Showstopper Restaurants
- Best Bars
- Shopping Spots
- Destination Hotels
- Spas
- Adrenaline Activities
- Places In The Sun
- Dubai Experiences
- Outside Of Dubai

Arabian Gulf

Das Island

Sir Bu Na'air Island

Dayyenah Island

Qarnyn Island

Zirku Island

Arzanah Island

Bu Tina Island

Halat Al Marbarraz

Saadiyat Island 19

Delma Island

Sir Bani Yas Island

10

ABU DHABI

Bu Kesheishah

Jebel Dhanna

Abu Al Abyadh

Ruwais

E11

Al Mirfa

Tarif

Ghayathi

Madinat Zayed

Sabkat Matti

Mezaira'a

Umm Hisn

Liwa Oasis

Arada

Hamim

Qasr Al Sarab
Desert Resort by Anantara 5

**KINGDOM OF
SAUDI ARABIA**

Rub Al Khali

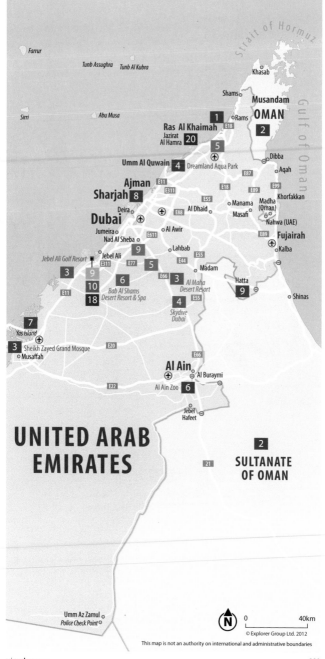

Farrur

Tunb Assughra   Tunb Al Kubra

Sirri   Abu Musa

Ras Al Khaimah [1]
Jazirat Al Hamra [20]

Shams

Khasab

Rams   [5]

Musandam
OMAN [2]

Dibba

Aqah

Umm Al Quwain [4] Dreamland Aqua Park

[E87]

Khorfakkan

Ajman [8]
Sharjah

[E311] [E18] [E89] [E99]

Manama   Madha (Oman)

Nahwa (UAE)

Dubai Deira

Jumeira

Nad Al Sheba

Al Dhaid   Masafi

[E88]

[E89] **Fujairah**

Kalba

[9]

Jebel Ali Golf Resort

[E611] Al Awir

Lahbab

[E55]

Jebel Ali [3] [9]

[E77] [5]

[E44] Madam

[E66]

[E311]

[10] [6]
[18] Bab Al Shams
Desert Resort & Spa

[3] Al Maha
Desert Resort

Hatta [9]

Shinas

[7]

Yas Island

[4] Skydive
Dubai

[E55]

[3] Sheikh Zayed Grand Mosque

Musaffah

[E20]

[E66]

Al Ain

Al Buraymi

[E22] Al Ain Zoo [6]

Jebel Hafeet

**UNITED ARAB
EMIRATES**

[2]

**SULTANATE
OF OMAN**

[21]

Umm Az Zamul
Police Check Point

Strait of Hormuz

Gulf of Oman

N   0   40km

© Explorer Group Ltd. 2012

This map is not an authority on international and administrative boundaries

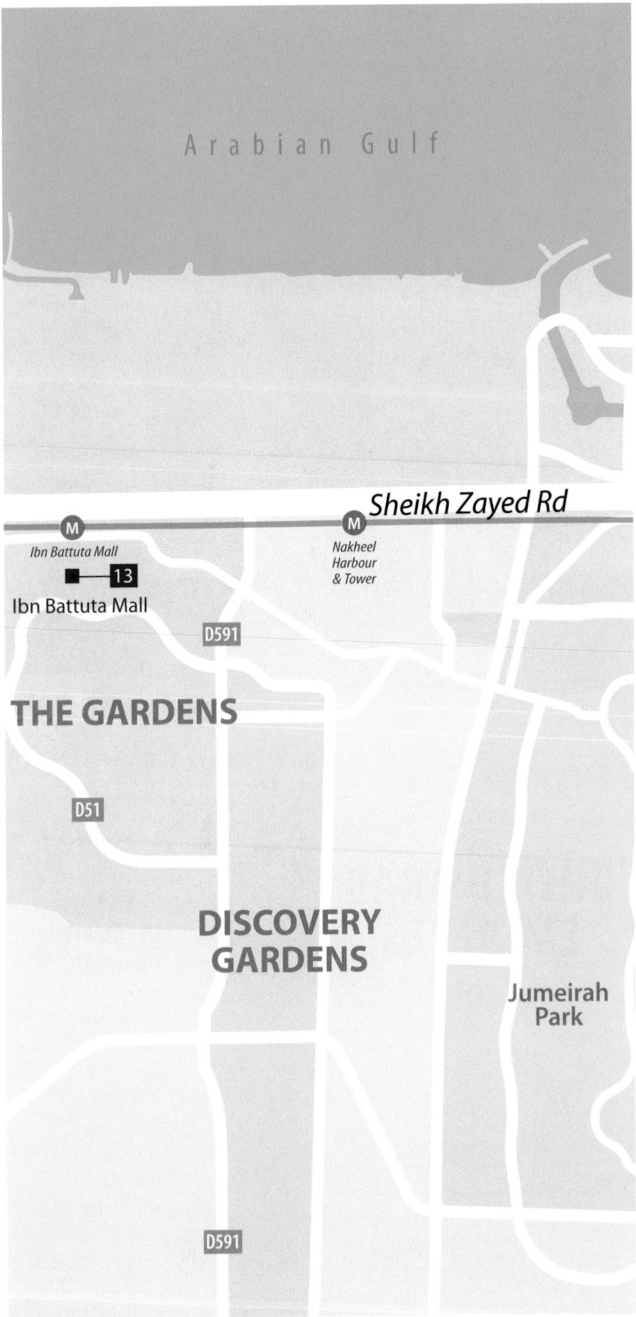

Arabian Gulf

Sheikh Zayed Rd

Ⓜ *Ibn Battuta Mall*

Ⓜ Nakheel
Harbour
& Tower

■ 13
Ibn Battuta Mall

D591

THE GARDENS

D51

**DISCOVERY
GARDENS**

Jumeirah
Park

D591

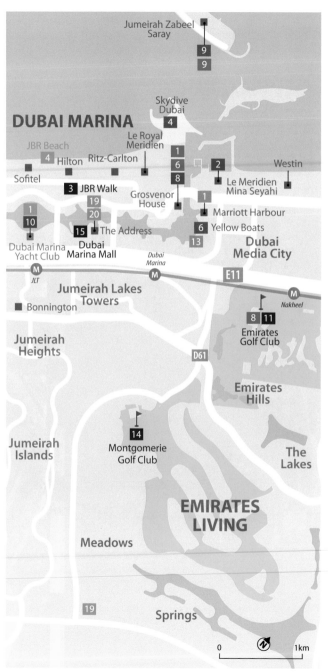

Jumeirah Zabeel
Saray

9
9

Skydive
Dubai

DUBAI MARINA

4

JBR Beach

4 Hilton   Le Royal
Meridien

Sofitel   Ritz-Carlton   **1**

3 JBR Walk   **6**

19   **8**

20   Grosvenor
House

15 The Address

Dubai
Marina Mall

1

10

Dubai Marina
Yacht Club

2
Westin

Le Meridien
Mina Seyahi

1
Marriott Harbour

6 Yellow Boats
13

**Dubai
Media City**

*Dubai
Marina*

M
JLT

M

E11

**Jumeirah Lakes
Towers**

Nakheel   **M**

Bonnington

8   **11**

**Emirates
Golf Club**

**Jumeirah
Heights**

D61

**Emirates
Hills**

**Jumeirah
Islands**

14

Montgomerie
Golf Club

**The
Lakes**

**EMIRATES
LIVING**

Meadows

19   **Springs**

0   1km

askexplorer.com

Trunk

PALM JUMEIRAH

One&Only
Royal Mirage

Al Sufouh Rd

Knowledge
Village

AL SUFOUH

Dubai
Internet City

DIC
Ⓜ *Sheikh Zayed Rd*

The
Greens

TECOM

AL BARSHA

Jebel Ali
Racecourse

Arabian Gulf

5
7
7

6
12

Burj Al Arab

7
10 1
3 10 1

Wild Wadi

1

8

Al Qasr

Souk Madinat

Madinat
Jumeirah

Jumeirah
Beach Hotel

UMM
AL SHEIF

Sharaf DG

Ⓜ

E11

Mall of the
Emirates

Ⓜ

Kempinski MOE

First Gulf Bank

Ⓜ

3
4
5
11
13
18

Mall of the
Emirates

Gold &
Diamond Park

18

0   1km

Arabian Gulf

Jumeirah Rd

UMM SUQEIM

Al Wasl Rd

AL MANARA

Sheikh Zayed Rd

Ⓜ Noor Islamic Bank

 3

Times
Square

AL QUOZ
INDUSTRIAL
AREA

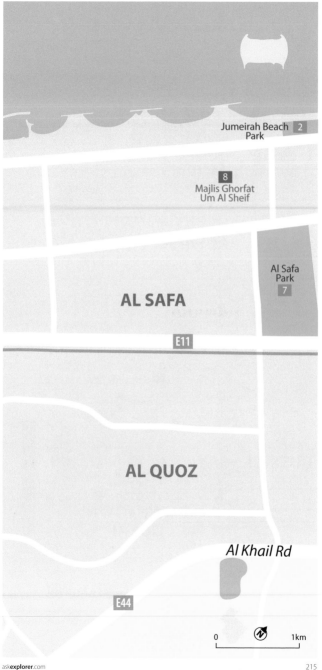

Jumeirah Beach Park 2

8
Majlis Ghorfat
Um Al Sheif

Al Safa
Park
7

AL SAFA

E11

AL QUOZ

Al Khail Rd

E44

0   1km

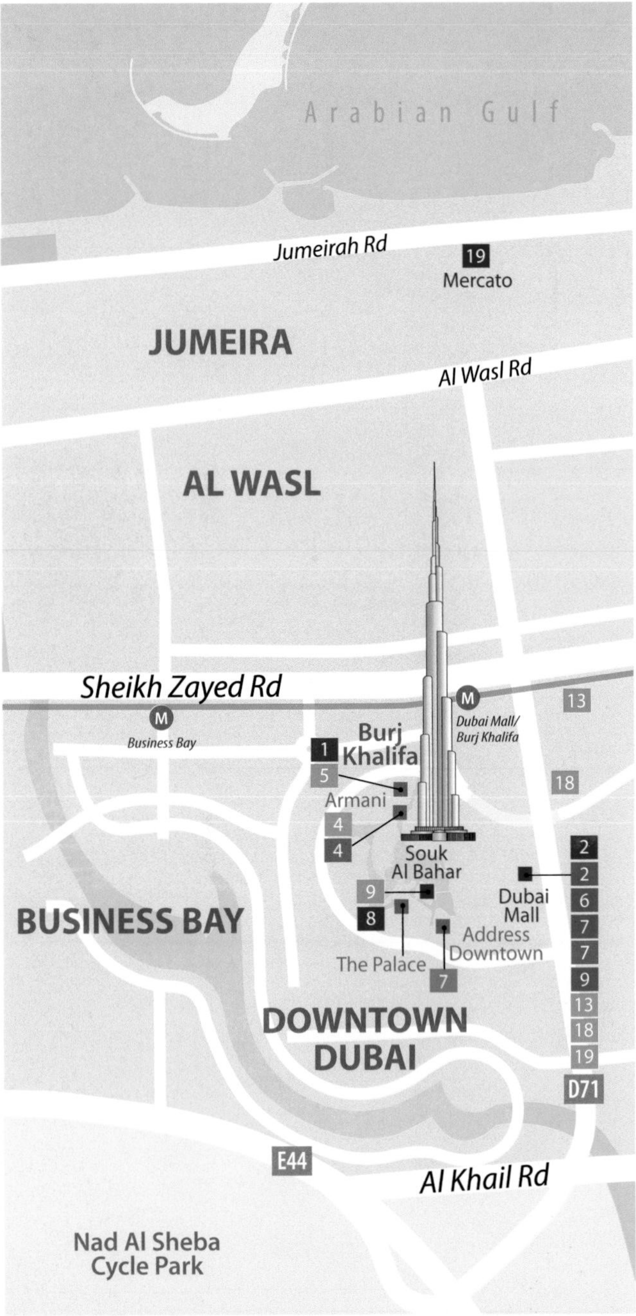

Arabian Gulf

Jumeirah Rd

19 Mercato

JUMEIRA

Al Wasl Rd

AL WASL

Sheikh Zayed Rd

Ⓜ Business Bay

Ⓜ *Dubai Mall/ Burj Khalifa*

13

Burj Khalifa

1
5

18

Armani

4
4

Souk Al Bahar

9
8

Dubai Mall

2
2
6
7
7
9
13
18
19
D71

The Palace

7

Address Downtown

BUSINESS BAY

DOWNTOWN DUBAI

E44

Al Khail Rd

Nad Al Sheba Cycle Park

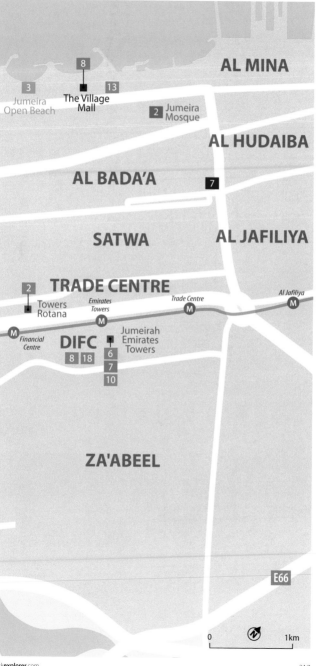

AL MINA

3 Jumeira Open Beach

8 The Village Mall

13

2 Jumeira Mosque

AL HUDAIBA

AL BADA'A

7

SATWA

AL JAFILIYA

TRADE CENTRE

2 Towers Rotana

Emirates Towers M

Trade Centre M

Al Jafiliya M

M Financial Centre

DIFC

8 18

Jumeirah Emirates Towers

6
7
10

ZA'ABEEL

E66

0   1km

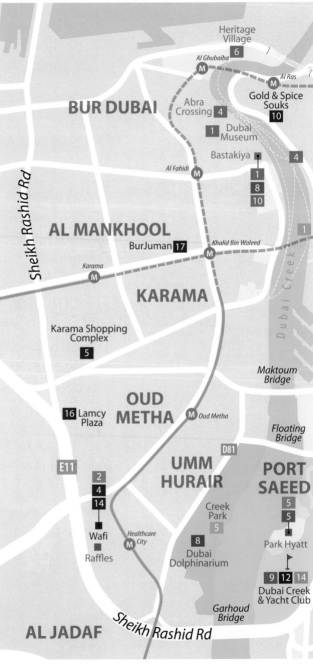

Heritage Village **6**

Al Ghubaiba Ⓜ

Al Ras Ⓜ

Gold & Spice Souks **10**

BUR DUBAI

Abra Crossing **4**

1 Dubai Museum

Bastakiya

4

1
8
10

Al Fahidi Ⓜ

1

AL MANKHOOL

BurJuman **17**

Khalid Bin Waleed Ⓜ

Karama Ⓜ

KARAMA

Karama Shopping Complex

5

Dubai Creek

OUD METHA

16 Lamcy Plaza

Oud Metha Ⓜ

Maktoum Bridge

Floating Bridge

E11

2
4
14

Wafi

Raffles

Healthcare City Ⓜ

UMM HURAIR

D81

PORT SAEED

5
5

Park Hyatt

Creek Park

5

8
Dubai Dolphinarium

9 **12** **14**
Dubai Creek & Yacht Club

Garhoud Bridge

AL JADAF

Sheikh Rashid Rd

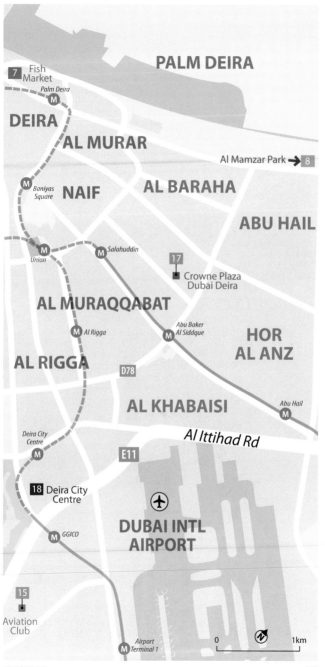

PALM DEIRA

7 Fish Market

Palm Deira Ⓜ

DEIRA

AL MURAR

Al Mamzar Park → 8

Ⓜ Baniyas Square

NAIF

AL BARAHA

ABU HAIL

Ⓜ Union

Ⓜ Salahuddin

17 Crowne Plaza Dubai Deira

AL MURAQQABAT

Ⓜ Al Rigga

Abu Baker Al Siddque Ⓜ

HOR AL ANZ

AL RIGGA

D78

AL KHABAISI

Abu Hail Ⓜ

Deira City Centre Ⓜ

Al Ittihad Rd

E11

18 Deira City Centre

✈

Ⓜ GGICO

DUBAI INTL AIRPORT

15 Aviation Club

Ⓜ Airport Terminal 1

0   🧭   1km

Al Khail Rd

E44

JUMEIRAH VILLAGE

Emirates Rd

E311

15
The ELS Golf Club

DUBAI SPORTS CITY

ARJAN

2 Dubai Autodrome

MOTOR CITY

Uptown Motor City

DUBAI STUDIO CITY

4
10

■
Dubai Polo & Equestrian Club

17
Arabian Ranches Golf Club

MUDON

Al Waha Villas

E611 Dubai Bypass Rd

Al Khail Rd   E44

AL BARSHA SOUTH

DUBIOTECH

MOHAMMED BIN RASHID GARDENS (PROPOSED)

19   *Emirates Rd*

ARABIAN RANCHES

E311

6

GLOBAL VILLAGE

0   1km

Drydock
Jaddaf   *Creek*   Ⓜ

Oud Metha Rd

E66

RAS AL KHOR

Dubai Creek

E44

Ras Al Khor Rd

**LAGOONS
(U/C)**

**RAS AL KHOR
IND**

**NAD
AL SHEBA**

**NAD
AL SHEBA**

Emirates Rd

**INTERNATIONAL
CITY**

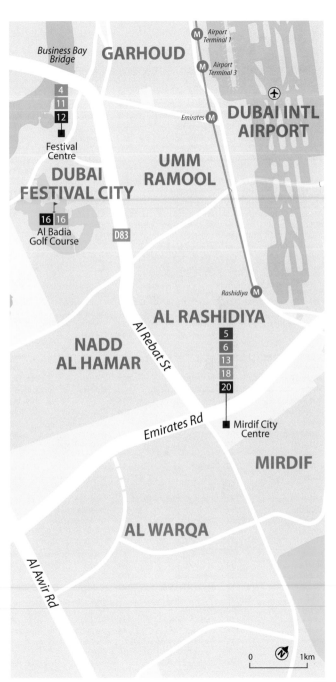

Index

USEFUL NUMBERS

Embassies & Consulates

Australian Consulate	04 508 7100
Bahrain Embassy	02 665 7500
British Embassy	04 309 4444
Canadian Consulate	04 314 5555
Chinese Consulate	04 394 4733
Czech Embassy	02 678 2800
Danish Consulate	04 348 0877
Egyptian Consulate	04 397 1122
French Embassy	02 443 5100
German Consulate	04 397 2333
Indian Consulate	04 397 1222
Iranian Consulate	04 344 4717
Irish Embassy	02 495 8200
Italian Consulate	04 331 4167
Japanese Consulate	04 331 9191
Jordanian Consulate	04 397 0500
Kuwaiti Consulate	04 397 8000
Lebanese Consulate	04 397 7450
Malaysian Embassy	02 448 2775
Netherlands Consulate	04 352 8700
New Zealand Consulate	04 331 7500
Norwegian Consulate	04 382 3880
Omani Consulate	04 397 1000
Pakistani Consulate	04 397 0412
Philippine Consulate	04 254 4331
Qatar Consulate	04 396 0444
Russian Consulate	04 223 1272
Saudi Arabian Consulate	04 397 9777
Spanish Embassy	02 626 9544
South African Consulate	04 397 5222
Sri Lankan Consulate	04 398 6535
Swedish Consulate	04 345 7716
Swiss Consulate	04 331 3542
Thai Consulate	04 348 9550
US Consulate General	04 311 6000

Emergency Services

Ambulance	998/999
DEWA Emergency	991
Dubai Police Emergency	999
Fire Department	997

Police Services

Department for Tourist Security	800 4438
Dubai Police	04 609 9999
Al Ameen (for neighbourhood problems)	800 4888
Dubai Police Information	800 7777

Road Service

Road service (AAA)	800 8181
MESAR Roadside Assistance	050 204 5208

24 Hour Pharmacy

Life Pharmacy	04 344 1122
IBN Sina Pharmacy	04 355 6909
Yara Pharmacy	04 222 5503

Hospitals

American Hospital	04 336 7777
Cedars Jebel Ali Int'l Hospital	04 881 4000
City Hospital	800 843 2489
Dubai Hospital	04 219 5000
Iranian Hospital	04 344 0250
Latifa Hospital	04 219 3000
Medcare Hospital	04 407 9100
Neuro Spinal Hospital	04 315 7887
Rashid Hospital	04 337 4000
Welcare Hospital	04 282 7788

Taxi Service

Al Arabia Taxi	800 272242
Cars Taxi	800 227789
Dubai Taxis	04 208 0808
Metro Taxi	600 566000
National Taxi	600 543322

Directory

Dubai International Airport	
Help Desk	04 224 5555
Flight Information	04 216 6666
Baggage Services	04 224 5383
Directory Enquiries (du)	199
du Contact Centre (mobile enquiries)	
From mobile	155
From any phone	055 567 8155
du Contact Centre (home enquiries)	04 390 5554
Directory Enquiries (Etisalat)	181
Etisalat Customer Care	101
Etisalat Information	144
International Operator Assistance	100
Mobile Phone Code (du)	055
Mobile Phone Code (Etisalat)	050/056
Speaking Clock	141
Dubai Meteorological Office	04 216 2218
Dubai Municipality Public Health Department	04 223 2323
Ministry Of Labour Hotline	800 665
Dubai Rent Committee	04 221 5555
Dubai Consumer Protection	600 54 5555
RTA Complaints Line	800 90 90
Salik	800 72545

BASIC ARABIC

General

Yes	*na'am*
No	*la*
Please	*min fadlak (m)*
	min fadliki (f)
Thank you	*shukran*
Please (in offering)	*tafaddal (m)*
	tafaddali (f)
Praise be to God	*al-hamdu l-illah*
God willing	*in shaa'a l-laah*

Greetings

Greeting (peace be upon you)	*as-salaamu alaykom*
Greeting (in reply)	*wa alaykom is salaam*
Good morning	*sabah il-khayr*
Good morning (in reply)	*sabah in-nuwr*
Good evening	*masa il-khayr*
Good evening (in reply)	*masa in-nuwr*
Hello	*marhaba*
Hello (in reply)	*marhabtayn*
How are you?	*kayf haalak (m) / kayf haalik (f)*
Fine, thank you	*zayn, shukran (m)/ zayna, shukran (f)*
Welcome	*ahlan wa sahlan*
Welcome (in reply)	*ahlan fiyk (m) / ahlan fiyki (f)*
Goodbye	*ma is-salaama*

Introductions

My name is...	*ismiy…*
What is your name?	*shuw ismak (m) / shuw ismik (f)*
Where are you from?	*min wayn inta (m) / min wayn inti (f)*
I am from…	*anaa min…*
America	*ameriki*
Britain	*braitani*
Europe	*oropi*
India	*al hindi*

Questions

How many / much?	*kam?*
Where?	*wayn?*
When?	*mataa?*
Which?	*ayy?*
How?	*kayf?*
What?	*shuw?*
Why?	*laysh?*
Who?	*miyn?*
To/for	*ila*
In/at	*fee*

From	*min*
And	*wa*
Also	*kamaan*
There isn't	*maa fee*

Taxi Or Car Related

Is this the road to...	*hadaa al tariyq ila...*
Stop	*kuf*
Right	*yamiyn*
Left	*yassar*
Straight ahead	*siydaa*
North	*shamaal*
South	*januwb*
East	*sharq*
West	*garb*
Turning	*mafraq*
First	*awwal*
Second	*thaaniy*
Road	*tariyq*
Street	*shaaria*
Roundabout	*duwwaar*
Signals	*ishaara*
Close to	*qarib min*
Petrol station	*mahattat betrol*
Sea/beach	*il bahar*
Mountain/s	*jabal/jibaal*
Desert	*al sahraa*
Airport	*mataar*
Hotel	*funduq*
Restaurant	*mata'am*
Slow down	*schway schway*

Accidents & Emergencies

Police	*al shurtaa*
Permit/licence	*rukhsaa*
Accident	*haadith*
Papers	*waraq*
Insurance	*ta'miyn*
Sorry	*aasif (m) / aasifa (f)*

Numbers

Zero	*sifr*
One	*waahad*
Two	*ithnayn*
Three	*thalatha*
Four	*arba'a*
Five	*khamsa*
Six	*sitta*
Seven	*saba'a*
Eight	*thamaanya*
Nine	*tiss'a*
Ten	*ashara*
Hundred	*miya*
Thousand	*alf*

Explorer Products

Residents' Guides

Mini Visitors' Guides

Photography Books & Calendars

Check out ask**explorer**.com

Maps

Adventure & Lifestyle Guides

Dubai Top Ten – 1st Edition

Lead editor Matt Warnock

Editorial team Jo Iivonen, Laura Coughlin, Rachel McArthur

Data managed by Ingrid Cupido

Sales by Bryan Anes, Sabrina Ahmed

Designed by Ieyad Charaf, Jayde Fernandes

Maps by Noushad Madathil

Photographs by Henry Hilos, Ieyad Charaf, Pamela Grist, Pete Maloney, Victor Romero

Publishing

Publisher Alistair MacKenzie
Associate Publisher Claire England

Editorial

Managing Editor Consumer Publishing
Matt Warnock
Editor Jo Iivonen
Corporate Editor Charlie Scott
Digital Projects Editor Rachel McArthur
Web Editor Laura Coughlin
Production Manager Therese Theron
Production Coordinator Kathryn Calderon
Editorial Assistants Amapola Castillo,
Ingrid Cupido

Design & Photography

Creative Director Pete Maloney
Art Director Ieyad Charaf
Contract Publishing Manager Chris Goldstraw
Designer Michael Estrada
Junior Designers Didith Hapiz, M. Shakkeer
Layout Manager Jayde Fernandes
Layout Designers Mansoor Ahmed,
Shawn Zuzarte
Cartography Manager Zainudheen Madathil
Cartographer Noushad Madathil
Photography Manager Pamela Grist
Image Editor Henry Hilos

Sales & Marketing

Group Media Sales Manager Peter Saxby
Media Sales Area Managers Adam Smith,
Bryan Anes, Dominic Keegan, Laura Zuffova,
Sabrina Ahmed
Digital Sales Area Manager James Gaubert
Business Development Manager Pouneh Hafizi
Corporate Solutions Account Manager
Vibeke Nurberg
Group Marketing & PR Manager Lindsay West
Senior Marketing Executive
Stuart L. Cunningham
Sales & Marketing Assistant Shedan Ebona
Group Retail Sales Manager Ivan Rodrigues
Retail Sales Coordinator Michelle Mascarenhas
Retail Sales Area Supervisors Ahmed Mainodin,
Firos Khan
Retail Sales Merchandisers Johny Mathew,
Shan Kumar
Retail Sales Drivers Shabsir Madathil,
Najumudeen K.I., Sujeer Khan
Warehouse Assistant Mohamed Haji

Finance & Administration

Administration Manager Fiona Hepher
Admin Assistant Joy San Buenaventura
Accountant Cherry Enriquez
Accounts Assistants Jeanette Carino Enecillo,
Joy Bermejo Belza, Sunil Suvarna
Public Relations Officer Rafi Jamal
Office Assistant Shafeer Ahamed

IT & Digital Solutions

Digital Solutions Manager Derrick Pereira
IT Manager R. Ajay

Contact Us

General Enquiries

We'd love to hear your thoughts and answer any questions you have about this book or any other Explorer product. Contact us at **info@askexplorer.com**

Careers

If you fancy yourself as an Explorer, send your CV (stating the position you're interested in) to **jobs@askexplorer.com**

Contract Publishing

For enquiries about Explorer's Contract Publishing arm and design services contact **contracts@askexplorer.com**

PR & Marketing

For PR and marketing enquiries contact **marketing@askexplorer.com**

Corporate Sales & Licensing

For bulk sales and customisation options, as well as licensing of this book or any Explorer product, contact **sales@askexplorer.com**

Advertising & Sponsorship

For advertising and sponsorship, contact **sales@askexplorer.com**

Explorer Publishing & Distribution
PO Box 34275, Dubai, United Arab Emirates
askexplorer.com

Phone: +971 (0)4 340 8805
Fax: +971 (0)4 340 8806